RATTLE OF A SIMPLE MAN

A Play in Three Acts

by

CHARLES DYER

SAMUEL FRENCH

LONDON
NEW YORK   TORONTO   SYDNEY   HOLLYWOOD

PRINTED AND BOUND IN GREAT BRITAIN BY
BUTLER & TANNER LTD.,
FROME AND LONDON

RATTLE OF A SIMPLE MAN

Presented by Michael Codron at the Garrick Theatre, London, on 19th September 1962, with the following cast of characters:

(in the order of their appearance)

CYRENNE	*Sheila Hancock*
PERCY	*Edward Woodward*
RICARD	*Daniel Moynihan*

Directed by DONALD McWHINNIE

Setting by VIC SYMONDS

The play is enacted during one night of the present year in Cyrenne's basement flatlet somewhere in London. The action is more or less continuous and is divided into three Acts with two Intervals.

Presented at the Booth Theatre, New York, on the 17th April 1963, with the following cast of characters:

(in the order of their appearance)

CYRENNE	*Tammy Grimes*
PERCY	*Edward Woodward*
RICARD	*George Segal*

Directed by DONALD MCWHINNIE

ACT I

SCENE—CYRENNE's *basement flatlet, somewhere in London. A night in winter.*

The flat is little more than a bed-sitter, but it is pleasant enough and quite posh—although the hanging light, which originally shone over the bed, has a piece of string pulling it to above the dressing-table. There are one or two slapdash touches like this. A basement atmosphere is obtained by the large window, C *of the wall* L, *and through here may be seen steps leading to the pavement above. A curtained opening* R *leads up a short flight of steps to a tiny, cluttered kitchen with a sink, dresser, Ascot water heater and gas cooker. There is a small window in the* R *wall. Up* LC *in the bedroom a door leads to a corridor, and when this is open the front door of the flat is visible up* L. *Below the window* L *two steps lead to a door to the dressing-room and toilet. On both doors there are coat-hooks. Up* R *in the bedroom is a tallboy. A large divan bed is* C, *and* L *of it is a table with a lamp and telephone. Down* RC *are a dressing-table, stool and waste-basket, and below these a record-player. A small portable electric fire stands down* RC. *There is a pouffe below the divan. Down* LC *is an armchair, with a small table below it, and in front of the window a flower-stand. In addition to the bedroom pendant there is a table-lamp, and there is another small hanging lamp in the kitchen. The light switch is* R *of the door up* L.*

(See Photograph and Plan of Set)

When the CURTAIN *rises the room and kitchen are in darkness, except for the moon through the window* R *and a street-lamp through the window* L. *A car door slams off* L, *and a taxi drives away. Two persons are descending the area steps, though we see only their legs—which pause half-way down.*

CYRENNE (*off*) Steady now, love. They're awfully steep. Perhaps you'd better wait until I've opened up. Or are you going to run out on me?

PERCY. No! (*Then a shade less definitely*) No, of course not.

*(*CYRENNE *gives a half laugh and moves from the window's view. We hear her key at a front door somewhere off up* L; *then she enters a hallway and opens the door of the room, switching on the lights)*

CYRENNE (*calling*) Well, come in, love!

*(*CYRENNE *is neither a Lamplight Lil nor a golden-hearted tart, nor is her voice scraping or scrunchy. She speaks nicely, and she is beautiful to see. Cyrenne is real—very real—and her moods are complex. In turn she is haughty, kindly—mocking, inviting or choosy—tempestuous or cold—earthy or prim—she is all these things. Her age could be twenty, but she might be as old as—oh, as any other woman! She switches on the bedside*

lamp, then crosses R *and starts the record-player. The music is quiet, soothing)*

(Calling) Come on! I shan't eat you. *(With her toe she clicks on the electric fire, then moves into the kitchen, turns on the light, and lights the gas under a kettle on the cooker. She returns to the bedroom, crosses to the window* L *and beckons)* Come along! Kettle's on.

*(*PERCY'S *legs move down the steps and* CYRENNE *draws the window curtains.*

PERCY enters up L. *He is an ordinary fellow, seeming about thirty-five. He has comic phases, some conscious and some unconscious—but he is far from being a clown. He is not really simple—he knows only too well his own limitations—and he uses an intense pride, a rocky dignity, to hide his sad fear that nobody wants or needs him. It takes a long time for his great natural charm to break through)*

Did you want a cup of tea, love?

PERCY. Er—no, I'm not bothered. Thanks all the same.

CYRENNE. Oh, all right. *(She hangs up her coat behind the door up* L, *which she closes, then goes into the kitchen and turns off the gas)*

*(*PERCY *has been celebrating some sporting event, as we see by his multi-coloured scarf, rosette and rattle. He is not drunk, however, just muzzy. Now, as* CYRENNE *busies herself in the kitchen, he takes in his surroundings and giggles to himself)*

PERCY. What a thing, eh! Jemima, what a—oogh. *(He sways slightly, placing a hand to his brow, and then, with much less bravado, adds)* Streuth! What a thing!

*(*CYRENNE *turns out the kitchen light and moves into the bedroom. She places her ear-rings and so forth on the dressing-table, then unzips her frock and steps out of it, wearing panties and a bra.* PERCY *is standing* LC, *clutching the rattle. He throws it on to the bed with a nervous laugh when* CYRENNE *looks at him. Then he thrusts his hands deep into his raincoat pockets and examines the carpet around his feet)*

Don't we sort of talk or anything?

CYRENNE. Why? *(She unplugs the record-player with her toe)*

(The music stops)

PERCY. Well, you know—I only thought—well—you know.

CYRENNE *(quizzically)* Change of heart, love?

PERCY *(bravely)* No! Not at all. I'm game for anything. *(He thrusts his hands even deeper into his pockets and edges half a step away)*

CYRENNE. And anything goes, eh, love? *(She folds her arms)* A spoonful of life; daring week-end in the wicked city?

PERCY. I've been in London before. Many times.

CYRENNE. Never done this before, though, have you!

PERCY *(defensively)* Yes.

CYRENNE. Have you?

Percy. Yes. 'Course I have!

Cyrenne (*smiling*) Scouts' honour? Okey-doke. (*She slides across the bed to his side, and yelps humorously when she momentarily sits on the rattle. Now she helps him off with his raincoat and places it, with his scarf, on the chair* L) Are you married?

Percy. Um—no.

Cyrenne (*looking at him*) No, you're not. Go on! I shan't look. (*She turns down the coverlet; and, without looking, passes the rattle to him*) Who won, incidentally?

Percy. Oh, don't ask! It was horrible. I reckon somebody covered the ball in grease; and as for the teams, they were so dead they should've carried flowers.

(*Silence for a while.* Cyrenne *moves her toy dog from the bed to the dressing-table; then she turns down the right-hand side of the bedclothes.* Percy *sneaks a look at her*)

Of course, the ground was too hard. Frosty. (*He clears his throat*)

Cyrenne (*looking up at him*) Don't be shy!

Percy. I'm not! I've seen hundreds of women.

Cyrenne. I've seen hundreds of men.

Percy. I suppose you must have, although you're not quite what I imagined—not at all. (*He takes his hands out of his pockets, then puts them back again*)

(Cyrenne *crosses to him*)

Few months ago, a gang of us were up in Morecambe. Phew! Saw a proper game there—only—local teams. . . .

(*His voice dies away as* Cyrenne *takes off his tie*)

Cyrenne. It's Percy, isn't it?

Percy. Yes. Percy Winthram. I'm from Manchester.

Cyrenne. Mine's Cyrenne. I was down in Manchester once: on a modelling job for one of the big stores.

Percy. It'd be Lewis's in Market Street.

Cyrenne (*placing his tie on the chair* L) May go down again some time.

Percy. Up! You go up to Manchester.

Cyrenne. Well, as long as you get there. (*He takes off his jacket*) It's a nice suit.

Percy. It's my best. 'Squite good quality.

Cyrenne (*with a sudden thought*) You do have money?

Percy. 'Course I have. Plenty.

Cyrenne. With you?

Percy. Yes. I brought out thirty pounds this morning.

Cyrenne. You won't need all that, Percy, unless you're staying the week. (*She lays his jacket on the chair* L, *then crosses to the bed-end and sits to put on her slippers*)

Percy. I've to be back on Monday morning. Win or lose, I promised I'd take mother to. . . . (*He stops*)

CYRENNE (*not unkindly*) All have mothers, don't you! Behind every man is a ma.

PERCY. Oh, that doesn't hold me back. I act like I please, don't worry! I'm—I'm thirty-five, you know.

CYRENNE. Oh, you must be—to have seen so many women. (*She watches him steadily*)

(PERCY *lowers his eyes to the floor and unfastens one shirt button. This takes ages*)

Would you rather I got ready first?

PERCY. No! No, I er—I. . . .

CYRENNE. One of us must make a move, dear. Take your pick!

PERCY. It—it just seems so cold-blooded like this.

CYRENNE. It's a matter of time, though, isn't it. We can't meet the family and go walks together. But *I* don't mind: nobody's forcing you to make love. If you prefer, I'll make a pot of tea and when you're ready you can scoot.

PERCY. I'm not. . . . (*He stops*)

CYRENNE. Not what?

PERCY. Not—not paying for nothing.

CYRENNE (*rising; flashing*) Now stop that, lovey! You pay for my time. I don't give a damn how you spend it; but you pay for it! (*She dons her black négligé from the hooks down* L)

PERCY. Oh, I feel umpty. I really do. (*He sits on the bed*) I've a head like a rocket-tail at blast-off. Oooo—(*He lies full length*)

CYRENNE. Well! What a come-down! Shaking his rattle; throwing his hat in the air! "See you tomorrow, lads! Don't tell mother: you'll make dad jealous! Up the Wrens!" Marvellous! (*Crossing up* L, *she locks the door and pockets the key*) I get the cash; and you get the key.

PERCY. Could I have a glass of cold water, please?

CYRENNE. Everybody's Romeo! Read next week's sizzling instalment! Oh, lady, you do pick 'em. And don't be sick over my bed! (*She fills a glass of water from the kitchen tap*)

PERCY (*sitting up*) I'm not that bad: glass of water and I'll be fine. Where did the rest of the lads go? Back to the digs?

CYRENNE. I've no idea; but you'd better think up some killer-diller tales: they're expecting great things from you. (*She hands him the glass of water*) Especially the one with red hair.

PERCY. That's Ginger—I mean, we call him Ginger. Did he go with the others?

CYRENNE. Maybe—after he fell off the taxi. (*She sits at her dressing-table*) He hung on the back for half a mile, yelling merry hell.

PERCY. I'm sorry if I've caused you any inconvenience.

CYRENNE. 'S all part of the racket. What's the time?

PERCY. Quarter past eleven.

(CYRENNE *makes a note in her diary*)

Why?

CYRENNE. Income tax. (*She grins, then gurgles merrily at his expression*)

PERCY. Why do you do this sort of thing, Cyrenne?

CYRENNE (*brushing her hair*) What sort of thing?

PERCY. Well—you know, live like you do. Oh, I imagine everyone asks you that.

CYRENNE. Usually bank managers who are writing plays; or Bible-punchers with helping hands—one of those calls every Thursday, with pale watery eyes, and begs to hear my problems. Oh, brother!

PERCY. He may be a kindly person who's genuinely interested in your welfare.

CYRENNE (*meekly*) Yes, Perci*val:* like the time he asked me to undress while he listened.

PERCY. Well, there was only genuine interest in *my* question. I'm not—not perverted or anything. I've no problems.

CYRENNE (*meaningly*) No?

PERCY. Now listen, miss. It was you approached me. You spoke to me in that club. *You* suggested this.

CYRENNE (*shrugging*) It didn't stop you coming.

PERCY. Only because I was merry. I was a bit merry. And now, if you must know, I'm very ashamed.

CYRENNE (*flinging down her hair brush*) Oh, you're ashamed!

PERCY. Yes. I feel awful about it.

(CYRENNE *rises angrily. She goes for Percy's jacket, scarf and raincoat and hurls them on to the bed; then returns to her stool* R)

CYRENNE. You're breaking my heart. Run and tell "the lads" all about your naughty night!

PERCY. You have the door-key.

(CYRENNE *throws the key on the floor and continues brushing her hair*)

Um—how er—how much do I pay?

CYRENNE. Auntie doesn't rob schoolboys. Leave a shilling and a piece of string on the mantelpiece.

PERCY. Why are you so peeved? (*He rises, bends to look for the key; and quickly flops down again. He rubs the back of his head, with a groan*) Oh—don't keep brushing your hair! Must you?

CYRENNE. Oh, rich. (*She drops the brush and swings round*) Are we married now or something? Whatever would your mummy say?

PERCY. It was scratching the backs of my eyes.

(CYRENNE *makes a sound of amusement. She rises, then hands him the glass of water from the floor by his feet*)

CYRENNE. *Shall* you tell mother all about your naughty night?

PERCY. No.

CYRENNE. Aw! What about the "lads"? (*She imitates his accent on* "*lads*") Shall you tell the lads?

PERCY. Probably.

CYRENNE. Everything? Exactly as it happened?

Percy. I suppose so.

Cyrenne. It won't be very exciting, will it! Yes, I can just see that pub in Manchester tomorrow night. Yup! (*She slaps her thigh*) There's Ginger an' Chalky an' Fred—and there's you in the middle, looking ashamed. "Eeee, I was so ashamed, Ginger," says Perci*val*. And Ginger says, "Eeee, I'm proud you were ashamed, Perci*val*." Then all the gentlemen join hands and yell: "Good old Percy! Pass the Bible!"

Percy. I must've offended you. I'm sorry if I did.

Cyrenne (*sitting beside him on the bed-end*) What will you say about me?

Percy. I'll say. . . . (*He changes his mind and sips water*)

Cyrenne (*quietly*) Yes, think about it. I often do—with fellows like you. Do they say, "I'm glad I didn't"—people like you, Percy? Or has the story grown by tomorrow? Dark brown chuckles and nudges in the ribs: "Ho, ho! What a night, chaps! What a night!"

(Percy *sips his water doggedly; but she nudges him*)

Percy?

Percy. We-ell—(*rising, he puts his tumbler on the table down* L) you see, I've never talked about things of—well, with a lady. I mean, you're so brassy with it.

Cyrenne. Won't you be brassy with Ginger?

Percy. That's between men.

Cyrenne. And this is between people. Aren't men people?

Percy. Yes, but—oh! D'you have an aspirin handy?

Cyrenne (*moving up* R *to the tallboy*) You still haven't told me how I come off in the expurgated edition. You know, the one you'll be so ashamed of.

Percy (*hotly*) Very well, I'll tell them the truth. I'll say I'm no good; I'm a flop. Satisfied?

Cyrenne. Then you've no call to be ashamed. (*She finds a bottle of aspirins in a tallboy drawer and brings them to him*)

Percy. There is a path between my ears full of little men with hammers. (*He sits down* L *and takes aspirins with a sip of water*)

(Cyrenne *drops a packet of cigarettes on the table beside him*)

Cyrenne. Help yourself.

Percy. No, thanks. I'm all smoked out. You know, you're a strange one, Cyrenne. I come here to—well, to—and end up with some kind of lecture.

Cyrenne. I'm intelligent, do you mind? (*She moves* C) It so happens I've travelled the world and I speak three languages. I passed through college with honours. I'm an M.A.—if you wish me to boast.

Percy. That's very good. Very good indeed.

Cyrenne. My father was a brigadier in the army. I was raised among people like that. Thirty pounds! I've spent more than your thirty pounds on—on a hat. (*Grandly*) Or a sudden whim, believe me!

Percy. Don't reckon any hat's worth thirty pounds. (*He rises; then meanders to the kitchen stairs, rubbing his hands briskly*) I didn't half drink some stuff tonight. Phew! I wondered if, um—(*he stops*) I wondered if. . . .

Cyrenne (*lounging on the bed*) What, love?

Percy. Nothing. (*He peers into the kitchen*) Is that a cupboard or something?

Cyrenne (*smiling faintly*) No.

Percy. Oh. (*He meanders back to his chair*)

Cyrenne (*blandly*) Why?

Percy. Nothing. I just wondered.

Cyrenne. I own this house: bought the mortgage. If I wished I could move upstairs. Just haven't bothered.

Percy. You're lucky. Wish I owned a house. (*He moves up* L, *opens the door, and looks into the small corridor beyond. Then he closes the door, returns down* L, *and points to the door down* L) Another room in there?

Cyrenne (*twinkling*) Yes.

Percy. Bathroom, is it?

Cyrenne. No. (*She lies back on the bed*)

Percy. Oh. (*He rubs his hands*)

Cyrenne. It's for luggage and odds and ends. A kind of dressing-room. There's a bathroom on the other side of it.

Percy. Oh! Would you excuse me, please.

(Percy *exits down* L, *rubbing his hands.*

Cyrenne *laughs to herself and rises. Picking up the key, she is about to replace it in the front door; then she pauses, weighing it thoughtfully in her hands. On an impulse she moves to the dressing-table and puts it in a powder bowl. Now she takes the rosette from Percy's raincoat and pins it on her dressing-gown. She admires the effect in her mirror; then puts his scarf round her neck, collects his rattle from the tallboy and moves* C, *twirling it.*

Percy *re-enters down* L)

Percy. You could have said straight away.

Cyrenne. You could have asked straight away.

Percy. It's not the sort of thing a gentleman does. (*He puts on his tie*)

Cyrenne. Up in Manchester.

Percy. Anywhere.

Cyrenne. Oh, we do it all the time in London.

Percy. You're just trying to make me look silly. You've been acting clever ever since I came. I admit I was wrong—somewhere along the line; but you did invite me here in the first place. (*He dons his jacket and throws his raincoat over a shoulder*) Could I have my things, please?

(CYRENNE *gives him the scarf and rattle, then pats the rosette*)

CYRENNE. Souvenir for Cyrenne?

PERCY. Mm? Oh. Yes. Yes, please have it. Oh—I'm not quite sure what we decided—with regard to terms.

(CYRENNE *ponders with assumed gravity*)

CYRENNE. Oh, I think all details being taken into consideration and with due regard to the culminating factors, we may safely assume—it's on the house!

PERCY (*laughing uncertainly*) Oh. Thank you very much.

CYRENNE. Not at all. (*She waves her hand in the air and lies back on the bed*)

PERCY. Well! I've enjoyed our little chat. (*He moves hesitantly to the door and turns*) I, er—I may not be up in London again for some while.

CYRENNE. Down!

PERCY. Pardon? Oh, yes: down in London. Been quite exciting— everything and all. And thanks for the glass of water and the aspirins. I can see that you're, um—well, a very nice kind of person.

CYRENNE. Underneath it all.

PERCY. No! I mean it! I've never talked to anyone quite so interesting. You don't meet many girls that are—that are, you know, original. And you are! Anyway.... (*He moves to the door up L and pauses quite a while with his hand on the door-knob. Then he comes back to Cyrenne, who is lying with her head hanging over the end of the bed and following a pattern on the carpet with her fingers*) You don't suppose Ginger could've—no, you say he fell off the taxi. (*He goes back to the door, then returns with a fresh thought*) Some of the other lads, though —maybe they're hanging around—waiting to see how I got on. Could be, you know. And—well, I've been so—so quick. You see?

CYRENNE. But we've nothing to be ashamed of—have we?

PERCY. Oh—no. No. (*He moves to the door, then turns again*) I er— I work in a cotton mill back home: in the Research Department, testing different tensilities; working on improved fabrics, you know. Nothing exactly scientific, but, um—are you listening?

CYRENNE. Yes.

PERCY (*moving down*) Hey! D'you know, I might've had something to do with that very dressing-gown you're wearing.

CYRENNE (*gravely*) Sort of makes you stop and want to think.

PERCY. Yes. (*He shakes his head sadly*) You know, Cyrenne, we come down here every year; and yet—once Saturday's finished, it's always dead for me. And tomorrow there's only the coach station— cold, early and Sunday-ish; chaps bragging about the women they've met, the beer they've drunk; then the long drive home with a headache. Not that I'm grumbling, you understand! There's always the girl-friend, you know. Oh, I've a very nice girl-friend. Oh, yes. I'm a happy man. I'm a very happy man. (*He looks at his watch*) Hey, d'you know it's only half past eleven?

CYRENNE. It is?

PERCY. Yes. It's early. Look—I'm not begging any favours, you know; but c-could—could I stay a bit longer, please?—as a friend— just to talk?

(CYRENNE *raises her head and looks at him. Then suddenly she swings off the bed and moves to the tallboy up* R. *From a drawer she takes a blouse. Throwing off her dressing-gown, she puts on the blouse. Then she says*)

CYRENNE. I may have people calling.

PERCY. Oh. Oh, I see.

CYRENNE. My sister and her husband.

PERCY (*more brightly*) Oh.

CYRENNE. He's a brilliant surgeon. They often call in for an hour. Sometimes they bring a whole crowd and we have a party. My sister's husband is very large—much broader than you, and he's tall with it. Nice man. I like him. Always decent with me. They're charming people, all of them. (*She takes the rosette from her dressing-gown and holds it against her blouse, surveying herself in the mirror*)

PERCY. They sound very nice. Very nice.

CYRENNE. They're not bound to call. 'Tisn't a definite arrangement. No! Doesn't match the blouse! (*She throws the rosette into a waste-basket and hurries out of the door down* L)

PERCY. Hey! That was meant as a keepsake: not to be thrown away. (*He crosses to the waste-basket and retrieves his rosette*) I'll have it back, seeing you're so pernickety. (*He moves to the door down* L *and shouts*) Best of luck to you, anyway! (*He strides to the door up* L, *stops, then walks slowly back again. Shouting*) I'll be off then. O.K.? Are you listening?

(CYRENNE *reappears suddenly, wearing skin-tight black trousers. She goes to the dressing-table and picks up her diary*)

What if they *don't* call?

CYRENNE. Someone's always popping in.

PERCY. You're not—going out again?

CYRENNE. No. (*She lies on the bed, with her toes on the pillow, and reads her diary*)

PERCY. Would you mind my stopping until somebody did call?

(CYRENNE *sighs indifferently and turns a page*)

Would you?

CYRENNE. Would I what?

PERCY (*irritably*) Can I stay until someone calls?

CYRENNE. Shouldn't you go to your hotel-or-whatever-it-is, and sober up?

PERCY. Who's drunk? I was never anything more than mellow— just a happy glow.

(CYRENNE *turns another page*)

Aw, I'm so walked on I'm getting a matt finish! (*He strides huffily to the door up* L, *finds it locked, and strides back again. He paces the bed area, muttering darkly, and then goes on his knees to look under the bed-end*)

(CYRENNE *leans her head right over, close to his*)

CYRENNE (*innocently*) Lost something?
PERCY. The key. You tossed it down. I can't see it.
CYRENNE. Hmm! You'd better go through the window. (*She returns to her diary*)
PERCY. Climb through?
CYRENNE. You could take a running jump.
PERCY. Through the window!
CYRENNE. Yes—open it first.

(PERCY *goes to the window* L)

And bring back a locksmith.
PERCY. At this hour! All we need is to unscrew that plate. I could do it in five minutes if you've a screwdriver.
CYRENNE. D'you expect me to spend five minutes with a screwdriver each time anyone calls?
PERCY. Well, you threw it on the floor! (*He pulls aside the curtains*) Hey, there're bars on the window!
CYRENNE. Squeeze through!
PERCY. Squeeze . . . ! A python'd be hard pressed.

(CYRENNE *flops back and, taking the weight on her shoulders, thrusts her legs up high. Then she does "developpes and entrechats" in the air*)

(*Turning and watching her*) You have, um—you have a very nice figure.
CYRENNE. I'm glad you like it.
PERCY. Quite—quite nice hair, too.

(CYRENNE *folds down into a sitting position. She smiles and nods towards the kitchen* R)

CYRENNE. Go put the kettle on!
PERCY. You mean . . . ? Oh, thanks! (*He throws his rattle into the chair down* L, *and crosses eagerly to the kitchen*) Yes, thank you very much. Ta. I'm most appreciative, I really am. (*He hangs his coat and scarf over the kitchen banisters*) Be all right here, will it?
CYRENNE (*surveying it lazily*) Move it—um, slightly to the left.

(PERCY *does so, then stops*)

PERCY. Why?
CYRENNE. Oh, it'll probably be all right.
PERCY. You don't half say some odd things, you do really. (*He moves into the kitchen, turns on the light, and fills the kettle at the sink*)

(CYRENNE *rises and looks at herself in the dressing-table mirror. She smoothes her hands down her body*)

CYRENNE. There's a tin of biscuits above your head and some blue cheese. Shall we have that?

PERCY. Oogh, yes. I am a bit peckish. (*He reaches down the transparent plastic biscuit tin*) Have you any more biscuits? There's only two.

CYRENNE. One each. Lovely!

PERCY. Oh. Yes.

(CYRENNE *moves into the kitchen and stands watching as* PERCY *prepares a tray with cheese, biscuits, butter and so forth*)

CYRENNE. My family home had a huge stone-flagged kitchen. Oh, it was a mansion, really—in Hampshire. As a child I remember the daffodils reaching my waist; and my arms wouldn't meet around the great white pillars of the portico. A white gleaming mansion, and we called it "Old Wob". I couldn't count the servants we had—old Pickles the butler, old Ned the chauffeur. . . .

(PERCY *is rinsing two cups under the tap*)

PERCY. I once stayed on a farm. Oh! I've wet your rent book.

(PERCY *takes a rent book from its hook above the sink and hands it to her.* CYRENNE *places it on a shelf over the cooker*)

CYRENNE. It's not mine, but thank you. My father was such a handsome man—so distinguished. You had to respect as well as love him.

PERCY. I imagine everyone respects a brigadier. Is he dead, then?

CYRENNE (*nodding*) He left all his money to my brother and me. My brother owns a country club.

PERCY. You're not half well connected! Was there much in the way of money?—if you'll pardon me asking.

CYRENNE. Ten thousand.

PERCY (*whistling*) A small fortune.

CYRENNE. It soon goes.

PERCY. No doubt you spent a lot buying this house.

CYRENNE. No, a man bought this for me. (*She stretches against the wall*) I could've had much more, but—well, you know.

PERCY (*disapproving*) I see.

(*The kettle whistles.* CYRENNE *turns off the gas*)

No! I'll do it, Cyrenne. I'll serve up. You go and sit down. Go on!

(CYRENNE *seems surprised. She backs away to the doorway*)

Go on! Scoot!

(CYRENNE *walks meekly to the end of the bed and sits, waiting.* PERCY *pours water into the teapot*)

I must remember what mother's always saying: pot to the kettle, never kettle to the pot. Ooogh, marvellous. It'll run round the room, this tea. (*He throws a towel over his arm, waiter-fashion; takes the teapot in one hand, the tray in his other; turns off the light with his shoulder—and goes to sit beside* CYRENNE) You know, I'm almost feeling healthy again. Must have been those aspirins. Mind you, my tongue still tastes like an old bath mat.

CYRENNE. Butter me a biscuit.

PERCY. Oh. All right. (*He does so*) Do you have normal meals?

(CYRENNE *bursts out laughing*)

What's up? What's the matter?

CYRENNE. No. They supply us with special food.

PERCY. I didn't mean it that way.

CYRENNE. Extra vitamins. Technicolored pills.

PERCY. I simply meant, well, some people—here's your biscuit.

CYRENNE. What about the cheese?

PERCY. Do your own cheese. You'll expect me to eat it next.

CYRENNE (*smiling*) Sorry.

(PERCY *butters his own biscuit, keeping his eyes to the task.* CYRENNE *bends her head down and looks at him*)

Sorry, love.

PERCY. You've nothing to be sorry for. I'm not sulking, you know. I don't sulk.

CYRENNE. Here! (*She cuts him a piece of cheese*)

PERCY. Ta. (*He takes it*) You see, it's hard to think of something to say without a double meaning—in the circumstances, so to speak. And we are in—well—peculiar circumstances.

CYRENNE (*gravely*) Oh, yes.

PERCY. I start to say something and all my sentences end in dots. When a character in a book sort of hesitates, you get dot-dot-dot-dot-dot. That's how I am.

CYRENNE (*nodding understandingly*) It's horrid for you.

PERCY. I suppose I'm just—(*he giggles a little*) just dotty. (*He laughs happily at this*)

(CYRENNE *smiles*)

I always laugh at my own jokes. I'm the only one who does.

CYRENNE. Never mind.

(*There is a longish pause while they munch their biscuits and cheese. Every so often he looks at her, then looks away when she returns his look*)

PERCY. I hope I'm not keeping you up.

(CYRENNE *shakes her head gravely, just managing not to laugh*)

PERCY. Is your mother still alive?

CYRENNE (*after a pause*) No.

PERCY. Ah. Perhaps she died when you were very young, then?

CYRENNE. Yes. Yes, indeed. I was twelve.

PERCY. Did your dad look after you?

CYRENNE. We had a nanny.

PERCY. Oh, yes, of course.

CYRENNE. Father was always away fighting.

PERCY. Fighting who?

CYRENNE (*shrugging*) He was away doing something.

PERCY. What regiment was your father, may I ask?

CYRENNE. Oh—cavalry. I didn't see him much. I spent my time painting and writing. I wrote a book when I was fourteen—thirty chapters. When I was twelve I—(*she stops*) something else happened. (*She rises suddenly*) I think I'll wear my jewellery. Just for you, Percy. Let's dress up. (*She picks up the tray and hurries towards the kitchen*)

PERCY. I'd have worn me medals if I'd known. (*He laughs*)

CYRENNE. How d'you mean? (*She pauses in the kitchen opening, seeming strangely tense*) What did you mean by that?

PERCY (*surprised*) It was a joke—just a joke.

CYRENNE. Oh. (*She laughs uncertainly*) Would you find my jewel box in the tallboy, please? (*She goes into the kitchen and puts the tray on the dresser*)

PERCY. Certainly. (*He goes to the tallboy up* R)

CYRENNE (*calling*) Oh, it may be the second drawer.

PERCY. What sort of box?

CYRENNE. A little white one.

> (PERCY *opens the second drawer and closes it again, standing away from it.*
>
> CYRENNE *returns from the kitchen, opens the drawer and finds her jewel box.*
>
> PERCY *doesn't quite know where to look. Watching him levelly,* CYRENNE *closes the drawer very slowly*)

Don't say you're *that* green!

PERCY. I'm a bachelor, you know.

CYRENNE. Yes. Now then. (*She sorts through the box*) Yes, let's have this one. (*Placing the box on the tallboy, she hands him a cheap chain-medallion; then turns her back for him to fasten it on*) I used to have lots of these but I sold them. Don't like memories. (*She turns round*) Nice?

PERCY. Yes, it's all right.

CYRENNE. I feel like dancing. Can you?

PERCY (*irritably*) Oh, yes. I used to run a dancing school.

CYRENNE (*laughing*) Really?

PERCY (*shaking his head*) I was joking. No, I wasn't even doing that. I was being sarcastic. Take no notice. (*He wanders* C)

CYRENNE. Are you still embarrassed?

PERCY. Don't be soft. I've been around. No, it's the way you say things. It wasn't "Shall we dance" or "Let's dance", it was "Can you?"

CYRENNE (*sitting on the end of the bed*) Not everybody *can* dance.

PERCY. Well, it so happens *I* can. You know, you make me feel as though I came up the Thames on a pogo stick. . . . Well, even if I did, it had a bell on—aw, forget it. I'm just grousing, I suppose. But each topic that crops up, you have a cupboardful: with your chauffeurs and white pillars, daffodils and Old Wob; brigadiers; money. You paint and you write. Thirty chapters at fourteen! Phew! I'm just about going under.

(CYRENNE *mooches to the dressing-table, her hands behind her back*)

CYRENNE. It wasn't a very good book: terrible immature.

PERCY. Premature'd be a better word. Thirty chapters! Takes me half an hour to sign a Christmas card.

CYRENNE (*sitting on the stool*) You do all this clever—research business.

PERCY. I only collate figures the Boffins have turned out. I collate them, you know. Oh, it's quite clever. I mean, I am clever at figures. But I don't suppose you'd want to spend the night adding figures together.

CYRENNE (*wickedly*) Not on paper!

(PERCY *says nothing to this, and she laughs*)

PERCY. I know what you mean. It's all right. There's another thing! I wouldn't dare say things to women at the mill that you say to me.

CYRENNE. You might have more fun if you did.

PERCY. I do very nicely, thank you. Oh, I realize it's very broad-minded and Bohemian but. . . . Not that I'm a prude. Don't get me wrong! I'm not a prude by a long chalk. I'm no angel. It's just that. . . . Phew! Early on I felt really exhilarated. It was the meshing —yes, the meshing of our personalities. But suddenly my ego's— well, it's squashed; it's beat; worse than that, it's bu—well, I won't be rude.

CYRENNE. Go on! I dare you!

PERCY. You know what I mean.

CYRENNE (*agreeing*) Mm. (*She sighs heavily, humorously*)

(PERCY *bites the edge of his thumb*)

PERCY. Oh—I'm no good with women. I'm like a chapel hat-peg. I'm everything the French laugh at in the English. (*He rises and follows a pattern on the carpet with his feet*) I told you a lie when I said I had a particular girl-friend. I haven't. I know lots of girls— no, I don't! Lots know me, let's put it that way. I can't explain why I've no steady girl. I'm old enough. Just never got round to it, I suppose. I'm kept pretty busy most of the time. Friday there's a get-together with the lads. You know.

CYRENNE (*nodding*) The lads. (*She imitates his accent, but without irony: with kindly acceptance, if anything*)

PERCY. Yes. Saturday's darts; Wednesday I spend with the Old Chilvington's—grammar school; Mondays I go to the pictures; and there's always television if the worst comes to the worst. The week goes by. I don't especially need anyone else.

CYRENNE. It's a problem, isn't it!

PERCY. No! That's what I'm explaining. I'm not moaning and

whining, I'm just talking. Why don't you say something? I'm very well off on the quiet; nice bit in the bank; and I shall eventually go abroad for the firm. (*He fishes a squashed, empty cigarette packet out of his pocket*) I shall have a secretary and a telephone.

CYRENNE. Take one of mine.

PERCY. No, thanks. I'm still full of feathers. (*He examines his face in the dressing-table mirror*) Beginning to need a shave, too.

CYRENNE (*rising*) There's only washing soap, but I can supply the rest. (*She takes a razor from her dressing-table*) It is a new blade.

PERCY (*moving* c) Who does it belong to?

CYRENNE. Me.

PERCY. Why should you have a—oh. Um. (*He backs hurriedly* L) It's kind of you, but I think I'll wait till morning.

CYRENNE. Your whiskers! (*She replaces the razor*)

PERCY. You don't want to watch me shaving.

CYRENNE. Yes, I do. I like it. It's manly.

PERCY. No, I prefer to wait, if you don't mind. I hate messing around in a shirt and collar. I like to strip off and get down to it.

CYRENNE. That's my boy! (*She smiles and crosses to* LC *with a saucy wink*)

PERCY (*near to blushing*) Oh, you're too sexy by far!

CYRENNE. Isn't it expected of me? (*She brings an ashtray from the table down* L *and empties it in the waste-paper basket* R)

PERCY. You're not so tough as you make out! (*He grins*) Mind you, there is a sort of X Certificate in the air—I'm just kidding! But it *is* a strange feeling being here. I mean *me!* Oh, you wouldn't understand.

CYRENNE (*bristling*) Because I'm different?

PERCY. Well, yes, you must be. I mean, I shall have tonight's atmosphere with me for—oh, for—well, I'll tell you: the other week I saw a dog run over. Poor little dachshund, it was; just lay in the gutter, yelping and screeching; everyone stood round, hoping it'd die quickly. And the chap who owned it—must have been six foot four—beefy fella, he was crying like a baby. Apparently it was a very old dog he was taking to be put to sleep; but the poor little thing jumped right out of his arms under this truck. It was going to die anyhow—but to think it had to go like *that!* All its legs crushed. (*He shudders*) I was cold inside for days. And yet tonight, after a fashion, I have the same kind of—*pungency*. Yes, that's the word. Pungency. But *you* wouldn't appreciate that.

CYRENNE. You think I have no feelings?

PERCY. Oh, yes, but our levels of sensitivity are. . . .

CYRENNE (*angrily*) Strange as it seems, I'm sad when a little dog dies.

PERCY. Yes, maybe, but. . . .

CYRENNE. I have salt in my tears just like you.

PERCY. I know. I know. . . .

CYRENNE. Then ram this past your halo, Percy. I'm no different to anyone else. I eat ordinary food, wear my best clothes in church, and never read dirty books at breakfast. Forget the dishes. Just blow!

PERCY. You don't half take offence!

CYRENNE. Here's the key of the door. (*She takes it from the bowl and lays it on the dressing-table*) "The lads" are waiting!

PERCY. Did you have it all the time, then?

(CYRENNE *covers her face with her hands*)

Are you crying?

(CYRENNE *shakes her head and gives a short defiant laugh. From the dressing-table she takes a woolly toy dog and holds it close to her cheek, as though it is an old friend-when-in-need*)

I shouldn't want to leave you—like this.

CYRENNE. Don't skin your nose! Everyone leaves me like this.

PERCY. I'll be happy to wash the pots, if you like.

CYRENNE. Some of them bluster, some of them swagger; but they mostly creep away.

PERCY. Or I'll attend to any odd jobs you may have outstanding. I'm in no hurry for an hour—if you have any squeaky floor-boards— faulty light switches—things that need oiling.

(CYRENNE *does not answer*)

I promise not to break anything.

(CYRENNE *laughs*)

CYRENNE. "He's good for me, Moma. He's awful good." That's a line from a book I once read. It was a book about a family in the Deep South, a family of rotters. All the Deep South families are rotters according to books and films. Have you noticed? Anyway, this girl used to get up in the morning, in the steaming heat, and. throw on a thin cotton dress and run into the forest.

PERCY. Was it a film?

CYRENNE. Don't know; but she didn't wash or anything: and she never wore knickers. I used to think it was terribly saucy, this teenage belle among all these sweaty men, guns, dogs—and no knickers. In one part she went swimming with a boy called Aaron; naturally they had no costumes either; and so she had a baby. Everyone hated Aaron because he wore boots or something; and when this baby came, the girl's brothers captured him in the forest.

PERCY. Yes, I think it was a film. I remember.

CYRENNE. And two of them held him down while the others kicked him in the stomach. I gave myself a headache crying. (*She rises*) Do you wear boots, Percy?

PERCY. Only for football.

(CYRENNE *laughs and moves up* R, *into the kitchen, turning on the light and taking an apron from the dresser*)

CYRENNE. And for hiking? Are you the type who camps out in summer?

PERCY (*following her into the kitchen*) I have done in my time, yes.

CYRENNE (*handing him the apron*) Mind your nice suit! Use the squeeze-in soap on the draining-board.

PERCY. Oh, lovely! Right you are, then!

(CYRENNE *helps him tie the apron*)

CYRENNE (*thoughtfully*) Are you a scoutmaster?

PERCY (*guiltily*) What—what would be wrong in that?

CYRENNE. Nothing. Use the towel you had before.

(*The telephone rings.* CYRENNE *enters the bedroom and lies on the bed to answer it*)

(*Into the receiver*) Yes? . . . Hello, Willie-darling! . . . All right; and you? (*She laughs intimately*)

(PERCY, *in the kitchen, listens jealously*)

. . . Well, you shouldn't run about with nothing on. . . . I did no such thing! . . . Oh, no, it was your idea! (*To Percy*) Don't break anything, will you, love?

PERCY. No.

CYRENNE (*into the receiver*) I wasn't talking to you, Willie . . . Yes. Jealous? . . . Mind your own business! . . . (*She laughs*) Go to a party tonight? . . . What sort of party?

(PERCY *pricks up his ears*)

. . . Yacht? What kind of yacht? . . . I've never been to a party on a yacht . . . Hang on!

(PERCY *has been disappointed by the turn of the telephone conversation. Now* CYRENNE *masks the receiver with her hand*)

(*To Percy*) Do you really want to stay awhile?

PERCY. I don't want to stop you having. . . .

CYRENNE. I asked you if you wanted to stay.

PERCY. Yes. But I mean. . . .

CYRENNE. Whatever happens?

PERCY. How d'you mean?

(CYRENNE *smiles*)

CYRENNE (*into the receiver*) No go, Willie! My boy-friend won't let me.

PERCY. No, wait a minute . . . !

CYRENNE. Ssssh! (*Into the receiver*) What did you say? . . . Oh, he's just a fella who does the washing up. G'-bye. (*She replaces the receiver*)

PERCY. Well! It's very nice of you.

(CYRENNE *rolls off the* L *side of the bed and picks up a tiny transistor radio from the bedside table*)

CYRENNE. It was only a friend of mine who has a motor-boat in Maidenhead.

PERCY. It might have been fun.

CYRENNE. I've been on the *Queen Mary*. Come on! Let's dance! Is that the correct phrase?

PERCY. Well. . . . there's all those dishes, you know.

CYRENNE. God! D'you call that entertainment? (*She moves* C) Come on, Man! I'm waiting. (*By now she has switched on the radio, which is blaring gay music—loud and swingy*)

(PERCY *enters from the kitchen, moves to her and tentatively takes her arms. He breaks away immediately*)

PERCY. It's no use. I can't. When the lads go dancing I stay in the bar.

CYRENNE. Well, I'm damned! (*She clicks off the radio and tosses it on the bed*) We have one hell of a scene because I say something wrong . . . !

PERCY. Yes, well, all right, I know! So I told a lie. I just wanted to be able to say I could do *something*—that's why.

(CYRENNE *crosses to the dressing-table and smoothes her eyebrows at the mirror*)

CYRENNE. I sacrificed champagne and oysters for you, love.

PERCY. Nobody twisted your arm. Why did you, anyway?

CYRENNE. Because I have clicking in the ears. I must have! Do you play tiddly-winks?

PERCY. No, I don't play tiddly-winks.

CYRENNE. You play darts, though.

PERCY. Yes. Why, have you got a board?

CYRENNE. Oh, no!

PERCY. More funny stuff. Very droll.

(CYRENNE *flops face down on to the bed. She feels the radio, and switches it on. Then she eases off the bed, carrying the radio, and sidles to Percy at* LC, *twisting her body in time to the music*)

CYRENNE. Well, Percival—(*she stands very close to him, her "motors" still running*) what *are* we going to do?

PERCY. Well—as I said before, those dishes don't get any cleaner. (*He backs away to* R *and hurries into the kitchen*)

CYRENNE *shrugs philosophically, turns the radio to full volume and does a hot little dance all by herself.* PERCY *steals a glance through the kitchen opening. After a couple of seconds, he grits his teeth and tentatively tries a few shuffling steps. He has as much rhythm as an ancient gong; but it shows promise.*

CURTAIN

ACT II

SCENE—*The same. A few minutes later.*

When the CURTAIN *rises,* CYRENNE *is teaching* PERCY *to dance. The radio is playing and they circle the room quite successfully—until Percy makes a wrong move.* CYRENNE *breaks away, limping painfully.*

CYRENNE. Damn and blast! (*She sits on the foot of the bed,* R, *takes off her slipper and rubs her foot*)
PERCY. Sorry.
CYRENNE. You have feet like a Yeti!
PERCY. Sorry.
CYRENNE. I'm crippled.
PERCY. Sorry.

(*The record ends and a foreign announcer jabbers away.* PERCY *laughs*)

What's he saying?
CYRENNE. How should I know? Switch it off.
PERCY (*switching it off*) I thought you spoke three languages.
CYRENNE. Only the swear words.
PERCY. It sounded like French.
CYRENNE (*replacing her slipper*) Come and talk to me.
PERCY. All right. (*He moves down and stands* R *of her*)
CYRENNE. Yes?
PERCY. Yes what?
CYRENNE. Yes what? Where are your manners? "Yes pardon!"
(*She tugs his arm*)

(PERCY *sits* R *of her on the bed*)

Go on, then! Start!
PERCY. Start what?
CYRENNE. Talking.
PERCY. You can't just start talking!
CYRENNE. Try! Say "I run a cotton factory". . . .
PERCY. I don't. I just work there.
CYRENNE. By yourself, or are there lots of people?
PERCY. Only about three thousand!
CYRENNE. All men?
PERCY. Phew! No! Only a third are men.
CYRENNE. There! We've started talking. Now, we have—oh, I can't add—say a thousand available women, at least. So, every day at the factory you rampage among a thousand juicy women.
PERCY. What's all this rampaging?
CYRENNE. Why not?
PERCY. I'm stuck in the lab most of the time.

CYRENNE. You stop for lunch.

PERCY. People don't rampage in the canteen! D'you think we have some kind of orgy during lunch break?

CYRENNE. Lovely! (*She slides from the bed to the floor*)

PERCY. Anyway, what're you driving at? I may not be going steady but I've taken girls out on dates. I've taken out plenty of girls.

CYRENNE. You've never slept with one.

(PERCY *is shocked. He gets to his feet*)

PERCY. Phew! I reckon you'd walk into Marks and Spencer's and shout Woolworth's! You don't know what I've done.

CYRENNE. Don't you think it's time you did?

PERCY. Who says I haven't?

(CYRENNE *smiles and shrugs*)

(*Capitulating*) All right I haven't! I never have. (*He crosses below her to* L) So you can laugh; laugh as much as you like.

CYRENNE. I'm not laughing.

PERCY. No, well . . . ! (*He runs his fingers along the back of the armchair* LC) I've had plenty of chances but I've never—followed them through. I don't have the technique, so Bob's your uncle. May I have one of your cigarettes now?

CYRENNE. 'Course.

(PERCY *moves to the dressing-table and takes a cigarette from her packet*)

PERCY. I live with the family, you see. I must get somewhere on my own. Time I did. You can't take friends back home, really. There's only the spare parlour; and even if I did, Mother'd make it a ceremony—fussing, bringing out the posh spoons, dressing up. I'm not grousing—me mother's a wonderful woman. Wonderful. But I once took home a girl called Cherry; just a friend, nothing more. But what a palaver! There's me mother twittering away, nudging me father—little sidelong looks at each other. I froze up. You see, you don't know if you want the posh spoons until—(*He lights his cigarette*) Anyway, I froze up.

CYRENNE. And Cherry?

PERCY (*grinning*) She crystallized! I didn't see her for dust.

CYRENNE. And all these other dates?

PERCY (*sitting* R *of her on the floor*) Well, if you've any advice it's most welcome, Cyrenne. Everything goes fine, you see, until near the end; then it's always the same—always the same long agonizing walk back to their gate. Truly agonizing, believe me! Talk about a dumb-bell—it has blood compared to me! I worry about this good-night kissing business all the way to the gate.

CYRENNE. Can't that wait till the next night?

PERCY. I'm afraid not. I never get a return match. No, it's the good-night kissing business. Mind you, I've done plenty of ordinary kissing; at parties and—well, just at parties, I suppose. But when I reach the gate and she says "Thanks for a nice evening", or some such phrase, and I know she's expecting—expecting me to get romantic; and—aw, the whole thing goes to pot.

CYRENNE. A lot of men find. . . . (*She changes her mind*) Why don't you let yourself go for once?

PERCY. Aye, I did try for once! The girl laughed; and she said—— (*He stops*)

CYRENNE. Said what?

PERCY (*obviously deeply hurt by this at the time*) —she said, "You'd better stick to training Boy Scouts, Percy." (*Defensively*) Yes, you guessed right. I am a scoutmaster. And I'm fed up feeling embarrassed when I tell people. Oh, life's a mess, it really is!

(*There is a slight pause*)

CYRENNE. It'll sort itself out and. . . .

PERCY. Anyway, I even asked Ginger. He's a smooth type, you know. He has one dance with a girl then disappears with her. Half an hour later he comes back looking smug and satisfied. So I asked him straight out. I said, "Whatd' you say to a woman when you've got her to yourself?" "Come on," he said, "I'll show you." He stopped the first girl he met in the corridor, and started making love to her!

CYRENNE. In the corridor?

PERCY. The neck of the man! Fantastic! Fantastic! Even with me there he went so far as to tell her. . . . Still, I'll not repeat it.

CYRENNE. Why, was it rude?

PERCY. Not really, but I can't tell *you*.

CYRENNE. Oh, come on, tell me.

PERCY (*squirming*) Well—well, he said—"What—what beautiful breasts you have." Now I feel a chump for telling you. (*Thoroughly embarrassed, he jumps to his feet and moves up* R, *then across to* L) There's nothing in it, I realize that. Everyone's broad-minded today. They talk openly about things my grandmother would've fainted at.

CYRENNE. Look—(*she sighs*) Percy, didn't your grandma have breasts?

PERCY. Well—eh?

CYRENNE. I know mine did. I remember she had a gigantic bust which entered a room several seconds before she did. She was proud of it. She was French—a marchioness—terribly old family. You're not old-fashioned, love—you're unbelievable.

PERCY. Well, I think *my* grandmother would've fainted.

CYRENNE. God help your grandpa's honeymoon!

PERCY. All right, pull my leg!

CYRENNE. Is this what Ginger meant by "Remember the top half"?

PERCY. When did he say that?

CYRENNE. He yelled it several times before he fell off the taxi.

PERCY. That's Ginger all over.

CYRENNE. But not you anywhere. A shame! (*She rises, pops her head over his shoulder and asks huskily*) Shall I order one pint of milk tomorrow, or two?

PERCY. Milk?

CYRENNE (*with a humorous sigh*) I'm afraid one'll be enough.

(PERCY *sits in the chair* L. *He removes the rattle from under him and places it on the table.* CYRENNE *goes into the kitchen for an empty milk bottle*)

PERCY. I'm not so pure as all that. I'm average.

CYRENNE. Stretching it a bit at thirty-five, don't you think? (*She crosses from the kitchen to the door up* L, *goes out, opens the front door, and puts out the milk bottle*)

PERCY (*strongly*) No, I don't. The people you meet aren't a true cross-section; not representative. I believe there're many folks like me who haven't the facets—yes, the facets. They haven't the facets to make friends easily. That doesn't mean they're warped or retarded, you know. There's nothing wrong with them. If anything. . . .

CYRENNE (*closing the door up* L *and moving to* C) Yes, I know! It's all my fault.

PERCY. Well, I don't go around doing peculiar things, you know; or writing on walls. (*He starts to laugh*)

CYRENNE. Now what?

PERCY. Oh, it's um—it's nothing.

CYRENNE. Percy, only nut-cases laugh at nothing; *and* it's terribly bad-mannered.

PERCY. I was, um—I was thinking about the mill canteen; and on one of the doors in the—well, in the Gentlemen's Room, d'you see—someone has written "A Happy New Year To all Our Readers"! (*He goes into ecstacies of merriment*) I think that's very funny, don't you?

CYRENNE (*dryly*) You must remember to tell Ginger.

PERCY. Yes. (*He laughs again*) No. It was Ginger told me. Oh, I'm sorry. It was rude.

(CYRENNE *smiles and kneels by his side*)

CYRENNE. You're very sweet, Percival—quite normal—and quite, quite untouchable. (*Suddenly, as though unable to keep her hands away from him, she scrubs at his chest and makes a loud comic growling sound. Then she rises and moves to* C, *stretching luxuriously*) Oooogh! Now I wish I'd gone to the yacht party. All at once I'm in the mood for wine, men and song.

PERCY. Oh, I'm batting at zero—and boring you in the bargain.

CYRENNE. Don't worry, my pet. Some woman'll materialize and your stuttering lips'll blossom into poetry. Where are those blasted tissues? (*She looks around the room*) She'll listen enraptured to your Lancashire sweet nothings. She'll come—and she won't laugh.

PERCY. She's taking a heck of a long time.

CYRENNE. At thirty-five! No, no! Beautiful age; everyone says so; beautiful! (*She goes into the kitchen*) Oh, she'll come from somewhere, sometime; maybe tomorrow; and you'll be in clover. (*She laughs*) I haven't thought as you do since I was twelve. I painted a picture of a naked boy when I was twelve. (*She switches off the kitchen light and comes back into the room*)

PERCY. I dare say we all. . . .

CYRENNE (*crossing to the tallboy*) From a model, love. I made him strip off and stand by an old water butt in the yard. He was—he lived in the same street. (*She laughs and opens a tallboy drawer, taking out the missing tissues; then she wipes her nose, throws the tissue into a waste-paper basket, and takes the box to the dressing-table*) Anyway, it rained and he caught a chill. Then I took the painting to school and caused a scandal—a riot in fact! You should have seen the teachers! Oh, it was delicious! They sent me home, called my parents. Reporters came—big splash in the local rag—altogether it was a bloody good do.

PERCY. Did you say "parents"?

CYRENNE. S-Stepmother. Father married again.

PERCY. You said you painted him by a water butt in a yard. A boy from the same street.

CYRENNE. That's right.

PERCY. I thought you lived in a big house.

CYRENNE (*hesitating*) I was staying with an aunt. She wasn't so well-off.

PERCY. I see.

CYRENNE. So, that was when I was twelve. By the time I reached sixteen I was really whooping it up.

PERCY. You must have had quite a life.

CYRENNE. Yes, sirree! (*She crosses to behind his chair*) Just fancy, though! Sweet thirty-five and still full of excitement and naughty thoughts. Never mind, pet. You're on top. (*Sadly, and full of yearning*) I can't even remember a first dance or a first kiss. Think I've been kissing and dancing since—God knows—since Adam.

PERCY. You're not so tremendously old.

CYRENNE. My story is twenty-four, Mr Winthram. A hundred and twenty-four, to you. I know. (*She moves to the side of his chair*) My old paint-box is still handy. Shall I paint you—in the raw?

PERCY. Oh. (*He laughs*) There's no-one I could show it to.

CYRENNE. I don't mean a picture. I mean paint *you*—all over. (*She tickles him energetically*)

(PERCY *goes into fits of anguished laughter*)

We'd use blue because you'd be cold and shocked, green for your past, and orange dabs for the blushes yet to come. (*Again she tickles him*)

(PERCY *rocks with laughter and begs her to cease*)

PERCY. Oh dear, oh dear, oh dear! (*He becomes suddenly serious*) Are you taking the mickey?

CYRENNE (*shaking her head and running a finger along his neck and round his ear*) No. I'm envying your carbolic-scrubbed life. D'you have Scout mistresses?

PERCY. In a way. We call them Guide leaders.

CYRENNE. Lean your head over.

PERCY. Mm?

CYRENNE. Against me. (*She sits on the arm of his chair, draws his head to her breast, and soothes his brow with her hand*) You're not missing much, love. Haven't you heard them say love is an overrated pastime? But—but if you really. . . . (*She pauses, then pushes him gently away and goes over to the bed*) No, I mustn't steal. (*She sits on the end of the bed and reaches for her diary*) It must have taken guts for you to come here tonight.

PERCY (*rising*) Frankly, I don't remember much; so I can't claim guts. Besides I'm glad. I'm—I'm damn glad, and I'd like you to know that.

CYRENNE. Yes, you've told me. I'm honoured.

PERCY. I mean it.

CYRENNE. So do I. It's All Souls' Night. Everyone loves everyone —everyone wears wings. (*She opens her diary*)

PERCY. Are you regretting missing the party?

CYRENNE (*looking up*) I'm pondering the alternative arrangements. You know, a performance indoors if it rains. (*She smiles*) But even the roof is leaking.

PERCY. Let's—let's get down to brass tacks. You're talking about making love to me, aren't you?

(CYRENNE *nods and gently mimics his accent*)

CYRENNE. Brass tacks.

(*On an impulse,* PERCY *goes and sits* L *of her*)

PERCY. I'd like to, Cyrenne. I-I'd like to. I'd like to kiss you . . . and hold you, and say things. Cyrenne, I want. . . . (*He makes a grab for her hand and, in doing so, knocks her diary to the floor. He looks at the fallen book, then turns away*) Oh, blast!

CYRENNE (*picking it up*) Doesn't matter. I'm always kicking it around.

(*But the moment has gone.* PERCY *intertwines his fingers and examines them*)

PERCY. Well, that's me: clumsy to the end! Bang on form!

CYRENNE. Never mind. (*Coaxing*) Percy?—Percival?

PERCY. I don't. I'm used to it.

CYRENNE. Where else did you go tonight? Mm? Come on, love. Snap out of the gloom.

PERCY. Last thing I remember's Piccadilly Circus: dancing in a ring round Eros. Then a policeman moves us on. Oh, yes! We went to a club next. Wait a minute! (*He racks his brains*) Yes! Phew!

Cigarettes ten bob! Ten bob for cigarettes! And Ginger! (*He laughs*) He was singing with the band. Next thing I remember's being thrown out. Then we went to your club and met you. . . . Hang on, though! Wait a minute! (*He rises, eyes wide*) Oh, Jemima! Now I've got it! We had a bet.

CYRENNE. You and Ginger?

PERCY. Yes. (*He backs away to* L) He bet me I wouldn't——

CYRENNE. —go home with me?

PERCY. Yes.

CYRENNE. How much?

PERCY. I've a dreadful feeling it was—(*He gulps*) fifty pounds.

CYRENNE. Including expenses? (*She is enjoying this*)

PERCY (*tragically*) Streuth! I must've been bonkers.

CYRENNE. You should be pleased. I am. I didn't know I was worth so much.

PERCY. Don't joke about it, please!

CYRENNE. You've won, haven't you? You're here!

PERCY. No, I haven't won. That's the whole point. It wasn't merely a question of coming home. I was supposed to. . . . Anyway, I haven't won.

CYRENNE. O-oh! Well now! (*She writes in her diary*)

PERCY. Cyrenne, seeing that. . . .

CYRENNE. It'll all be forgotten by tomorrow.

PERCY. It won't, you know! Borrow threepence from Ginger and he's waiting with his hand out next day. Very strong principles, has Ginger.

CYRENNE (*still writing*) So you'll have to tell a fib after all.

PERCY. I couldn't now. No point in making a bet if you don't stick to the bargain. Oh, this is horrible. (*He paces in silence*) This is *horrible!*

CYRENNE (*angrily*) Look, if you find me so damned horrible, go lick your wounds somewhere else!

PERCY. I'm sorry: I didn't intend any. . . .

CYRENNE. Just phone a cab, Percy. It's late; I'm tired; and you're worried.

PERCY (*hotly*) Oh, it's always me! (*He strides to the telephone up* L)

CYRENNE (*quietly*) There's a taxi number on the light switch.

(PERCY *dials a number.* CYRENNE *reads aloud from her diary*)

"Saturday. Eleven-fifteen. Met Percy Winthram. Exclamation mark! Talked of life and disappointments. Felt someone looking over my shoulder for the first time in years. Exclamation mark!"

PERCY. Cyrenne. . . .

CYRENNE. Sssh! No.

PERCY. Oh, heck!

CYRENNE. "I wonder what will become of him; and if he'll think of me? Cue for song." (*She throws the diary behind her on to the bed; then rises and moves down* L) Any luck?

PERCY. It's ringing.

CYRENNE. They'll answer. Let yourself out, love. And next time you date a girl, try forcing your luck.

(CYRENNE *goes out down* L.
PERCY *hangs up. He dials a fresh number, after consulting a card taken from his pocket*)

PERCY (*into the receiver*) Hello? Is that the Pablo Private Hotel, please? . . . Oh. This is Mr Winthram. Has Mr Grappley returned yet, please? . . . Thank you. (*He waits impatiently, saying to himself*) I'm fighting time now; and I'm too damn scared to wind the clock. Oh, what if he's not back? What if he's plastered down some alley? (*Into the receiver*) Hello, Ginger? It's Perce. . . . *Perce!* . . . Fine. I got on fine. . . . I er, came *home* with her, yes. . . . Yes. . . . Talking. . . . It's all so far, yes. . . . Ginge, listen! Don't you think it's a bit stupid all this?. . . . I'm not backing out at all. Frankly, I'm giving *you* a chance. I mean, I'm here. I'm *here*, Ginge. Just a matter of time, that's all. . . . Hello? . . . D'you still want to go through with it, then? . . . Who's dead scared. Ha! . . . Hello? . . . Hello? . . . Ginger? . . . (*He hangs up gloomily*) Fool! Stupid fool! Throwing his money around! Fifty pounds on a damn stupid bet.

(CYRENNE *enters down* L. *She has changed into a stylish electric-blue cocktail dress, and she seems altogether more acceptable and pacific*)

CYRENNE. Still here?

(PERCY *rises quickly. He stares at her*)

PERCY. The taxi number didn't answer.
CYRENNE. Make yourself useful, then. Zip me up, there's a sweet. (*She pauses at* C)

(PERCY *comes down to her*)

PERCY. Where're you going?
CYRENNE. Going back to the club.
PERCY (*struggling with the zip*) Phew! It's an awkward zip.
CYRENNE. Only going up. . . . Well done! (*She moves to her tallboy; and we see that her dress is ninety per cent backless, with a tiny ten per cent zip. She opens her jewellery box and extracts a bracelet*)
PERCY. I rang up Ginger.
CYRENNE. Did you?
PERCY. Yes. Oh, I owe you fourpence. (*Moving to the bedside table, he gets out four pennies and puts them down on it*)
CYRENNE (*holding out her arm across the bed*) More help, please.
PERCY (*putting on the bracelet*) Don't you want to hear what he said?
CYRENNE. If you like.
PERCY. He wouldn't give up the bet.
CYRENNE. You know Ginger! Thank you. (*She crosses to the dressing-table and dabs perfume on her wrists*)
PERCY. Shall you be seeing anyone special?

CYRENNE. Probably.

PERCY. You look nice.

CYRENNE. Do I?

PERCY. Oh, what's the matter? Everything's gone—I don't know. Is it because I said "horrible"?

CYRENNE. No, that's forgotten.

PERCY. If you're cheesed because I messed up your evening— I'm sorry. Honestly. I'm so clumsy, so flipping clumsy.

CYRENNE. No, you're not.

PERCY. Then why have you gone so cold?

(CYRENNE *take his hand, smiles at him sadly. Then the moment passes*)

CYRENNE. But we don't *really* mix now, do we! Not really. So you're going to Euston and I'm going to see where they buried Saint Pancras.

(CYRENNE *pats his hand and releases it*)

PERCY. Cy-Cyrenne, I had butterflies all yesterday thinking of the trip down here. I kept remembering: "It's a holiday tomorrow. A holiday!" So why shouldn't I make it one? If—if you'll be as you were before. If you'll be warm: you know—warm—I think this time I could. . . .

(*The doorbell rings. They both turn.* PERCY *slaps his fist in plaintive frustration*)

PERCY. Oh, why did it have to ring now! (*Urgently*) I mustn't —I can't miss my chance. If you'd only be friendly again. . . .

(*The doorbell rings.* CYRENNE *moves to the dressing-table and picks up the door-key*)

CYRENNE. Well, once you get in the fresh air. . . .

(*Again the doorbell. She hands the key to Percy, crossing him to down* L)

Open up, love, before they break in.

(CYRENNE *exits down* L)

PERCY. Ee, I wish I were different. (*He unlocks and opens the door, then moves into the corridor. He opens the front door*)

(RICARD *enters. He is a handsome Latin type in his late twenties. Perhaps there is a trace of weakness in his face. He is changeable—excitable —very much like Cyrenne, in fact. He ignores Percy and moves into the room. He crosses immediately to the kitchen, taking in his surroundings en route*)

PERCY. I'm er, pleased to meet you.

(RICARD *peers into the kitchen, then calls*)

RICARD. Cinny! Cinny!

(CYRENNE *hurries in down* L)

CYRENNE. Ricky! Ricky-love! (*She runs to him*) What a surprise.
RICARD (*to Percy*) Would you mind? This is personal.
PERCY. Oh, er. . . .
RICARD. These yours? (*Without waiting for an answer, he takes Percy's clothes from the banisters* R *and throws them across at him*)
PERCY. Hey! Just a moment . . . !
CYRENNE (*crossing to Percy up* L) Friend of the family, Percy. Excuse his bad manners.
PERCY. Is this how it ends, then?
CYRENNE (*indifferently*) 'Fraid so, sweetie. Good luck with Ginger.
PERCY. Night-night. (*To Ricard*) Night-night

(PERCY *makes a lonely exit.*
CYRENNE *turns to face Ricard*)

CYRENNE. Any time you're passing, just pop in and kick out my friends.
RICARD. Friend, was he!
CYRENNE. That's right—friend. (*She laughs lightly*) You know, this is fantastic. You stroll in after all this time—don't even toot your horn—just stroll in. (*She moves to him*) How've you been, Ricky?
RICARD (*turning away slightly*) Fine. You?
CYRENNE (*merrily*) Things have happened; time's gone. . . .
RICARD (*interrupting impatiently*) I've come from moma and dad, Sis. Said I'd take you back tonight.
CYRENNE. Oh?
RICARD. They want to see you. They're opening a new restaurant. We're all going in—whole family. Me, Margo—and we need you as well.
CYRENNE. I've given up slaving in cafés, Ricky. No, thanks.
RICARD (*in the same dull, stubborn tone*) You can be manager; then we shan't have to go outside the family.
CYRENNE. Dad can manage it. You don't need me.
RICARD. I just promised you'd go back and talk to them.
CYRENNE. Ah! We're not talking very much these days, the family and me.
RICARD. Dad was very eager to have you. . . .
CYRENNE (*strongly*) He's not my father.
RICARD. All right, stepfather then. Where's your coat? I'm taking you back, Sis. (*He looks round the room, then crosses to the hooks up* L)
CYRENNE. Just like that! Marvellous!
RICARD. You need only stop an hour; then I've done my bit. (*Unhooking her coat*) This the one?
CYRENNE. Are they all there? Auntie Bo, Uncle Arturo, everyone?
RICARD (*moving to her*) Aunt Bo's baby-sitting for Margo and me.
CYRENNE. Spaghetti's out, Ricky—got that? And I'm not attending any cookhouse conventions at this hour.

RICARD. No? What *were* your plans for tonight, Sis?

CYRENNE (*looking at him for a moment, then turning away up* L) I spent my childhood in our old café and the very mention of cooking and cafés makes me ill.

RICARD. Well, anyway—tell *them*. (*He moves to her, holding up the coat*)

CYRENNE. No. I said no!

RICARD. Come on!

(RICARD *pulls her arm with the intention of helping her into her coat, but she pushes him away. A struggle develops between them, half brother-sister fight and half serious. It ends violently. They fall across the bed and* CYRENNE *strikes at his face and frees herself; then she rises and backs away, panting*)

RICARD (*clutching his cheek*) You little bitch!

CYRENNE. So I'm not going anywhere tonight (*she re-hangs her coat behind the door*) not anywhere.

RICARD (*rising*) Not even on the prowl, Sis? On the beat?

(CYRENNE *swings round, shocked*)

I *know*, Sis. I've seen you. Hadn't been off the ship a day! First person I met was old Tosky and he said, "I've seen your sister picking up men in a drinking club." I thanked him with a belt in the jaw. I was insulted. (*He laughs shortly*) So to prove he was lying, I watched outside that club of yours. I've watched for the last few days.

CYRENNE. That's a decent brotherly gesture.

RICARD. Were *you* decent, bringing men home? Two men, one after another! I was sick, physically sick. (*Cruelly*) Been out tonight, have you?

CYRENNE (*almost hissing*) Yes.

RICARD (*shouting*) Fine! Good! I'm glad! Holy Mother, why d'you do it? Why did you start?

CYRENNE (*shaking her head dully*) It's like I said: things've happened.

RICARD. My own sister—a prostitute.

(CYRENNE *turns on him. Her voice is low, fierce, quivering with emotion*)

CYRENNE. Now listen, Ricky: you come into my house—this *is* my house—and you don't even ask how I am. You b-be good to me, Ricky.

RICARD. Oh, yes. I've every reason, of course. (*He picks a news-paper off the tallboy and toys with it*)

CYRENNE. Well, you're not so clever! You go abroad for months on end leaving a wife and two kids.

RICARD (*moving* C) I went on a job; and I've made money . . . good, *clean*, money.

CYRENNE (*shouting*) Don't say "clean" to me! You don't know Ricky. You don't *know*. (*She moves behind the chair* L) But since you're

c

so damned sanctimonious, I'll tell you. Yes, why not! It was *him*, Ricky. He barged into my room and—and I was dressing.

RICARD. Who barged in?

CYRENNE. Moma took his side, as usual, but I'd done nothing . . .

RICARD. Who barged in?

CYRENNE. Dad. He was always like that with me. In the old café —that tiny kitchen—when he used to squeeze past me. And even upstairs.

RICARD. You're making it up. You're making it up to excuse yourself.

CYRENNE (*moving to him at* c) No, Ricky: it was popa . . .

RICARD. Stop it, Sis! You're lying again.

CYRENNE. I never lied to you, Ricky. Honest! I never . . .

RICARD. Will you button up! (*He pushes her so that she falls across the end of the bed. Then he beats her across her back with the rolled newspaper. He strikes her five or six times, then throws down the paper and moves to the window* L) Aw, get up, Cinny. I didn't hurt you that much.

CYRENNE. No, you're not so tough. (*She rises and moves to the dressing-table*) I don't blame you getting your own back. But try it once more and I'll tear your eyes out! (*She grabs the woolly dog from her dressing-table and hurls it across the room at her brother*)

(RICARD *catches it. They face each other across the bed, and suddenly exchange a faint smile*)

RICARD. Well, there's no call to set your dog on me!

CYRENNE. His name is Chikita.

RICARD. It's a bitch-of-a-dog. Hiyah, Chikita! (*He hurls it back at her*)

CYRENNE. Hey! Don't hurt him.

RICARD. Aw, Sis . . . !

(*On a mutual impulse, they meet and embrace, kneeling in the centre of the bed. Then they assume a casual conversational tone*)

CYRENNE. When did you get back?

RICARD. Last week. Been working at popa's café.

CYRENNE. This new restaurant your idea?

RICARD. Mm. I'm putting up the cash. S'going to be real snooty, Sis. Drinks, pianist, everything.

CYRENNE. Well, bully for you!

RICARD. They were all down there tonight, talking about it; saying how wonderful if Cinny came back. And Uncle Arturo— well, you know how excited he gets—said, "Let's pay a visit. Let's-a pay da visita pronto," he said. So I said *I'd* come. I saw them all arriving here and finding you—with someone, perhaps. It would have killed moma.

CYRENNE (*tonelessly*) Oh, yes. Yes, it would.

RICARD. I haven't told them, you know; not even Margo.

CYRENNE (*lightly*) Good. Thank you.

RICARD. Cinny, come and stay at moma's tonight, eh? Just for me. Well—well, hell! We were always fighting or crying together—always pretty damn close. Eh, Cinny?

CYRENNE. I can't. (*She shakes her head*) I can't.

RICARD. I'm sorry about—about the way things are; sorry I walloped you.

CYRENNE. I wanted to marry you when I was young. I used to tell people: "I'm going to marry Ricky when I grow up."

RICARD. Remember when you almost hacked off my wrist making us blood brothers?

CYRENNE (*shrugging*) I happened to catch a vein.

RICARD. Yeah. (*He examines his wrist*)

CYRENNE. I thought it'd hurt less if I used a blunt edge. It was the thing for taking Boy Scouts out of horses' hooves.

RICARD. Remember when you painted that picture of me and took it to school?

CYRENNE. Oh—that. I got a hell of a lecture from moma about brothers and sisters: what they were allowed to do and what they were not allowed to do.

RICARD. Moma?

CYRENNE (*nodding*) She was quite different with me after that. She never took her eyes off me. Moma had me in the old café every possible minute—washing up, scraping leavings into that filthy tea-chest in the yard—do you remember the steam beetles on the oven wall?

RICARD. No.

CYRENNE. I do. Once I dropped my cloth behind the stove pipe and when I pulled out my hand it was covered in steam beetles. (*She shudders*) It was my punishment, you see, Ricky.

(RICARD *starts an impatient denial but she interrupts, nodding gravely*)

You know what she thought, what everyone thought? Oh, yes. Moma made herself very clear—even at my age.

(RICARD *swings off the bed to* L. *He speaks strongly—almost violently, and one wonders if he is protesting to hide a conscience*)

RICARD. So I undressed while my own sister painted my picture: so what! I was only—I wasn't fourteen. I've led an ordinary, normal, healthy life. I've married; I have kids; Margo has no complaints. Anyway, it's past—forgotten. I don't know why I'm yapping.

CYRENNE. It started to rain and you wanted to go in; but I wouldn't let you. (*Rising, to meet him below* C) So you ran and tattled to moma. You were always a tell-tale, Ricky. Used to like seeing me punished, didn't you, boy!

RICARD. Are you saying this is how it all started?

CYRENNE. Perhaps.

RICARD. Bringing me into it?

CYRENNE. "Perhaps" to that as well.

RICARD (*crossing her to* R) Oh, great! Now it's *my* fault!

CYRENNE. I said "perhaps". (*Angrily*) But it might help if you remembered it next time you call, instead of worrying about how you feel—how the family feels—how everyone feels except *me!* Oh, what the hell! I know you mean well, love. (*Impulsively she kisses him*) I know you mean well. Want a drink?

RICARD (*nodding*) Like I'm buried in sand!

CYRENNE. You bring the bottle, I'll fetch the glasses.

(CYRENNE *goes into the kitchen, switching on the light, and collecting the tumblers from the dresser.* RICARD *moves to the tallboy for the whisky*)

Oh, I've got some stamps for little Ricky and Perry.

RICARD. Oh good, thanks. (*He uncorks the whisky and puts it on the dressing-table*)

CYRENNE. One of the g—a girl friend gave them me. I'd told her I had two nephews.

RICARD. Thanks.

CYRENNE. Margo at the café? (*She switches off the light, returns to the bedroom with the glasses and pours two tots*)

RICARD. Yes. Lunch-times. . . . Thanks, that's plenty. (*He moves away to* C *with his glass*)

CYRENNE. Chow!

RICARD. Chow!

(*They drink.*
      CYRENNE *puts down her glass on the dressing-table and hunts through various pots and boxes on her dressing-table—in search for the foreign stamps. Then she pauses, speaking to him over her shoulder*)

CYRENNE. Supposing—supposing I tried, Ricky?—No more lies and putting on airs; just plain, respectable me.

RICARD. Would you, Sis?

CYRENNE. Not spaghetti again: I couldn't try that saintly hard. Go in an office, maybe: nine till five and tennis afterwards. (*She faces him*) That make you happy?

RICARD. 'Course it would.

CYRENNE. All right then, it's a deal. (*She spits on her hand and holds it out*) Moko Poko!

RICARD. Poko magee!

(*He spits on his hand, they clap twice, then shake. It is obviously some secret childhood ritual. She holds his hand for a second then quickly turns away and continues searching*)

CYRENNE. Where are those stamps? Tell you what! I'll bring them round tomorrow.

RICARD (*putting his glass on the dressing-table*) To my place?

CYRENNE. Yes. I haven't seen your kids in ages.

RICARD (*uneasily*) It's a bit difficult tomorrow, Sis. (*He moves* C *and sits on the pouffe*)

CYRENNE. Monday then. (*Rummaging*) Where *are* they!

RICARD. Trouble is Margo isn't. . . .

CYRENNE. Here they are! I'll make a huge parcel with these in the centre. (*She sorts through them*)

RICARD. Don't go to any bother. Shall I take them?

CYRENNE. No, I want to see their faces.

RICARD. Only—you know Margo. She likes them in bed early and they're at school during the day.

CYRENNE. Any time suits me.

RICARD. It's only that um—the next few days—um, let's see now. (*He avoids looking in her direction*)

(CYRENNE *is getting the message. She turns slowly and looks at him*)

CYRENNE (*evenly and deliberately*) How about next Friday at six?

RICARD. Margo's folks are coming, I think.

CYRENNE. Saturday?

RICARD. Well—I'll think about it, eh?

(CYRENNE *holds a hand to her mouth, tightly closing her eyes. She moves up* R, *a tremble in her voice*)

CYRENNE. What am I s-saying! (*She forces a laugh*) I'm—I'm going away next week.

RICARD. You are?

CYRENNE. Switzerland. Winter sports. Yes. I've a boy-friend—Percival. (*She collects her glass from the dressing-table*) He's just dying to take me on holiday. All above-board—no hanky-panky with Percy. He was here when you arrived.

RICARD (*rising*) Well, this is wonderful, Sis. Marvellous.

CYRENNE. Yes. (*She sits at her dressing-table*) He's not a bad fellow; wants to marry me; always popping the question. He knows all about me.

RICARD. Well, what do you know! Cinny, why not? Eh? (*He claps his hands gaily*) And I'll be best man.

CYRENNE. Mm.

RICARD (*heartily*) You know, I've just thought—Friday would've been fine. Margo's folks aren't coming until. . . .

CYRENNE. Don't push it, Ricky! (*In a whisper*) I got the message. (*She drains her glass*) Buzz off now, love.

(RICARD *moves up for his coat, then comes down behind her*)

RICARD. This on the level, this holiday?

CYRENNE. Switzerland. Yes.

RICARD. Honest? I mean, all above-board and. . . .

CYRENNE. I've had all I can take, Ricky.

RICARD. It's a fair question if you really mean to change.

(CYRENNE *feels humiliated*)

CYRENNE (*in a quiet, dead voice*) I'll keep myself clean—wash my hands and nails. I'll send you a doctor's report.

RICARD. Aw, cut the music, Sis! I'm only asking for your word —your word of honour, that this Percy fella is. . . .

CYRENNE (*rebelling against this, and shouting*) No! It's a lie. He's a nasty sordid gentleman who calls every Saturday. And I'll be in next Saturday when he calls—and the next after that.

RICARD (*yelling in return*) And what about us? What when someone else says he's seen my sister? I can't break everybody's head.

CYRENNE (*rising*) Try praying for me!

RICARD. It's a bit bloody late for that now.

    (CYRENNE *pushes past him to* L. *He tries to catch her arm, but she shakes him away*)

CYRENNE. Leave me alone, Ricky.

RICARD. All I'm asking is your word that. . . .

CYRENNE. Will you leave me alone! Just leave me alone, will you? (*She is mentally beaten. She gives in and sobs, resting against the wall* L *and saying repeatedly*) Ricky, leave me alone. . . .

    (RICARD *exits up* L.

      CYRENNE *hears the door slam, and turns. On the table down* L *she sees Percy's rattle. She moves to it, fondles it for a second or so, then drops it into the chair. She moves to the bed, flops down, and hugs her toy dog*)

I don't need them. I don't need anyone.

    (*The telephone rings. Eagerly she clutches the receiver to her ear*)

Yes? . . . Yes. . . . Willie-darling, hello! . . . Starting out for where? . . . No, thanks, love. I've been on the *Queen Mary*. (*Urgently*) Come round here instead. . . . *Please*, Willie. *Please*. Come and see me, Willie. *Please* come over. . . . You'll be seasick! . . . Yes. (*Dully*) Some other time. (*She hangs up and wanders to the dressing-table. There she sits on her stool*)

    (*The doorbell rings*)

(*Calling*) It's not locked. (*She hurriedly repairs her make-up*)

    (PERCY *enters up* L)

PERCY. I forgot my rattle.

    (CYRENNE *tries to laugh; but tears flow instead. She weeps silently*)

It isn't half cold, I've been round the block six times. No, seven. A policeman followed me last time round. Can I come in and get it? My rattle?

    (CYRENNE *nods her head.* PERCY *closes the door and moves down to above the armchair* L)

'Tisn't half cold. I saw two of the lads from our charabanc. Phew! Talked about sloshed! Their eyeballs were bottle shaped. I bet that copper's nabbed 'em by now. Hey, what's the matter?

CYRENNE. Nerves, I think.

PERCY (*crossing to her*) Was it that chap?

CYRENNE (*shaking her head*) It was my brother.

PERCY. Your brother? Oh, yes, he's the doctor. Oh, no—your brother runs the country club.

CYRENNE. He works in a café. It's my—it's a restaurant.

PERCY. We-ell, country club sounds better. We all put on airs, you know.

CYRENNE. Not you, Percy! You don't.

PERCY. Everyone. Our old man at the mill can hardly talk for the plums in his mouth; but nobody minds; he's a good enough boss. He's never afraid to admit he came from Wigan. There's a story going the rounds. Shall I tell you?

CYRENNE. Funny one?

PERCY. It's a tale—you know, a joke. I'm quite good at jokes. It might cheer you up.

CYRENNE. I doubt it—oh, I'm sorry—go on. Try.

PERCY. Well—(*he clears his throat*) the managing director's wife called on the boss's wife, you see. Our boss's wife, I'm talking about. (*He shifts from foot to foot during this tale, delivering it as a party piece. He couldn't tell a joke to save his life*) And the boss was in the garden; gardening. And he shouted out: "Ethel!" His wife's called Ethel. I mean that's her name in real life. Anyway. . . . Wait a minute! Let me get it straight. Um—yes. The boss called out: "Ethel! Where's the manure for the roses?" It's not near the knuckle. (*He looks at her*)

CYRENNE. Who said that?

PERCY. No, the joke isn't. It's a bit cheeky but—oh, I'll think of another.

CYRENNE. No. I like this one. I'm fascinated.

PERCY. Oh. Well, he shouted: "Ethel! Where's the manure for the roses?" and the managing director's wife said: "Oh, Ethel! Can't you make your husband say 'fertilizer'? It's much more refined." And the boss's wife said. . . . (*He giggles*)

CYRENNE. Said what?

PERCY. "Make him say fertilizer! It's taken me ten years to make him say manure!" (*He roars with laughter*)

(CYRENNE *ponders the joke unenlightened.* PERCY's *laughter slowly fades as he notices her puzzlement*)

Don't you get it?

CYRENNE. I thought fertilizer and manure were the same thing.

PERCY. They are! But don't you see—he'd always called it . . . ! Oh heck! I'm really up against the dots now. (*He scratches his head*)

CYRENNE. Percy! It's only a piece of wood on a ratchet.

PERCY. Beg pardon?

CYRENNE. This rattle.

PERCY (*nodding*) Yes, it was an excuse. (*He sits on the corner of the bed*) D'you ever talk to yourself? I do. If I'm not feeling particularly sleepy at night, I go long walks round the town. And I talk to myself. Sometimes, if I haven't finished the conversation when I get back home, I go round again!

(Cyrenne *smiles*)

Oh, I do! Anyway, tonight—round and round that block, I was talking to you. And this is what I said: if it's y-your—d-desire to go with men; I mean, you as a woman *do* go. . . . (*He blurts out*) You went cold with me. You lost interest. Surely I'm not so dull that even you—oh, it's no use. It sounds wrong. (*Urgently*) Cyrenne, can't you realize what tonight has been like for me? I'm walking through Market Square, say, at three a.m. And suddenly there's a gigantic building slap-bang where the chip shop was—I mean, it shouldn't be there! But it is. I open the door and there's a million people I've never met. They're all smiling and they seem to want me. Lights ablaze; music blaring. And then an exciting woman— (*He looks at her*) a sweet, wonderful, exciting woman grabs my hand and hurtles me into the middle of it all. Three o'clock in the morning! And you thought there was nothing ahead but the eight o'clock buzzer. (*Sadly*) Do you think I'm daft?

Cyrenne. Probably. (*She touches his hand*) Are you still hungry?

Percy (*rising*) Have you found some more biscuits?

Cyrenne (*rising*) I've some beans, sausage, corned beef, and more beans. Would you fancy those?

Percy. Can a duck swim!

Cyrenne. There's still those damn dishes.

Percy. The devil with them! You'll not see me for spray. (*He throws his raincoat on the bed and hurries into the kitchen switching on the lights*)

(Cyrenne *follows him in and fastens the apron round him.*
Percy *turns on the taps and starts into the dishes with gusto*)

Cyrenne. Lot of money, fifty pounds.

Percy. Ee, d'you have to rub it in? I'm still bleeding.

Cyrenne. A fellow could have himself a crazy holiday on fifty.

Percy. I only spent thirty at Morecambe.

Cyrenne. Yes. Two crazy people could almost go. (*She places her finger-tips to her lips and backs out of the kitchen. She sits at her dressing-table, watching herself in the mirror*) This girl in the building-that-never-was, would you take her on holiday?

Percy. I'd need to be quick: due back at the mill on Monday.

Cyrenne. Why? Would the mill close without you?

Percy. Ha! That'll be the day.

Cyrenne. Mmmm. . . .

Percy. You may think me strange, but I enjoy washing up. I get quite a kick out of it. I like it. Most folks can't bear the sight of dirty dishes. Not me! I love it. Must be the cosiest thing in the world to have a little kitchen all your own. . . .

He prattles happily away.

CURTAIN

ACT III

SCENE—*The same. Half an hour later.*
There is a tray of stacked dishes on the pouffe, below the end of the bed.

When the CURTAIN *rises,* PERCY *and* CYRENNE *are kneeling on the bed, facing one another, an orange balanced between their foreheads. Both are holding glasses and* CYRENNE *also has the whisky bottle. They are by no means drunk—not even "high"; but they are, perhaps, floating a little.*

PERCY. —Idea is to travel it around our heads, turning as we go. People have rolled it miles. One who eats it, wins.
CYRENNE. To win this, you'd need a square head—*and* horizontal teeth.

(The orange falls. They laugh. PERCY *sits on the end of the bed)*

PERCY *(pointing to the tray)* Hey, that was the best corned-beef-bolognaise I've ever had. Didn't realize I was so peckish. Were you peckish?
CYRENNE. Ah was that! Liqueur, Monsewer? *(She pours whisky into his glass)*
PERCY. Ta! I'm glad it turned out well: it's the first corned-beef-bolognaise I ever cooked. *(He drinks)* You don't do much cooking, then?
CYRENNE. Not if I see it coming. *(She raises her glass)* Skol!
PERCY. Arrivederci!
CYRENNE. May as well finish it. *(She empties the bottle into their glasses)* Dead men tell no tales.
PERCY. Hey up! Steady on!
CYRENNE. Now, Percival! Don't tell me you were boasting about all that liquor you drank.
PERCY. No, I had plenty—but I'm a beer-man m'self. I once drank fourteen pints at a sitting.
CYRENNE. What happened?
PERCY. I passed out. *(He grins sheepishly)* Oh, Cyrenne, I know what I was going to ask you—oops! *(He slides from the bed to the floor)* What college did you attend?
CYRENNE *(off guard)* College?
PERCY. You said you got an M.A.
CYRENNE. Oxford.
PERCY. University, eh! Which one?
CYRENNE. One for girls, naturally.
PERCY. Magdalene?
CYRENNE *(sipping her whisky)* Mm.
PERCY. Did you get an M.A. for languages?

CYRENNE (*shrugging*) Various courses. I only went for fun; never did any work. Young people should have fun.

PERCY. Within reason.

CYRENNE. I did. It was all singing, dancing, and parties on the river bank. Sometimes a whole gang of us'd take out a punt and float, just float, with bottles of wine and meat pies. (*She giggles*) David—he was an earl's son—once got the pole stuck, and we floated on leaving him like a monkey up a stick in the middle of the water.

(*This is obviously something she has read in "Girls' Own", but* PERCY *is tremendously impressed*)

PERCY. Aye, must have been marvellous at university.

CYRENNE. He was a nice healthy boy. (*Wistfully*) No—complications. He gave me his fraternity pin. (*She is mixing up some American college film she has seen. She balances the whisky bottle on her head*) He had freckles and close-cropped hair, and cuddly big sweaters with stripes round the arms and "Great Britain" on the front. During semester he played trombone with a jazz group.

PERCY. What's semester?

CYRENNE (*vaguely*) Oh, you know. And when I was bored we'd race down the lanes in his car, me steering and him working the pedals and playing his trombone. He wanted to marry me; but I told him he was too young. Poor David! He sulked for weeks. (*Her voice trembles slightly with emotion. She empties her whisky glass in one gulp*) Anyway, he wasn't supposed to go with girls. It ruined his baseball or something.

PERCY. Baseball? At Oxford?

CYRENNE (*smoothly*) He was American. They have baseball teams for Americans at Oxford.

PERCY. Son of an earl?

CYRENNE. That—was David. I was talking about Philip.

PERCY. Oh. I must've lost track some place. But how did you get an M.A. if you never did any work?

CYRENNE. Father bought it.

PERCY. Bought an M.A.! That doesn't seem right.

CYRENNE. You can do anything with money. Father was never short. When ever he came to see me he always pushed a fiver in my hand. "Have fun, sweetie," he'd say.

PERCY. He sounds a very grand person. Shame he died so early: he might have—well, helped.

CYRENNE. Oh, never mind. (*She gets off the bed and rubs her back with the whisky bottle*) Aaagh—ni-ieece!

PERCY (*ponderously*) Cyrenne, do you think, perhaps, you had too much—too soon?

CYRENNE (*smiling*) And you did it without a couch! (*She puts the bottle on the tray and tosses a cushion from the floor on to the chair down* L)

PERCY (*rising*) I can imagine what it's like to have been to university and all that; then strike a bit of bad luck. (*He takes out his wallet*) So I thought—seeing your father isn't around—don't be

insulted—but—(*He thrusts a five-pound note at her self-consciously*)
Have fun, sweetie! Ha ha!

CYRENNE. What's it for?

PERCY. Nothing. No strings. Go ahead!

CYRENNE (*taking it; slowly*) I'm afraid you've crept up behind me,
Percival.

PERCY. Oh, it's for my own sake as much as anyone. Makes me
feel good. First time I've ever walked beside white pillars; first time
I ever felt important. (*He turns away to* R, *looking at his wallet*) Not
that I agree with throwing money around. Ee heck! I can't have
spent all that! Phew! Must've been those clubs.

CYRENNE. That's how it goes. (*She moves across to him and gives him
back the money*)

PERCY (*taking it automatically*) Thanks. (*He is about to replace it in
his wallet, when he realizes*) No! Oh, no! What's gone is gone. That's
yours.

CYRENNE. O.K. (*She takes it back and, crossing him, goes to hide the
money in a pot on the dressing-table. She turns and tentatively offers it to him,
with an instinctive jerk-back of her hand before he could even have touched it*)
There's still time.

PERCY. No, no. Just spend it wisely and—aw! Spend it how you
like. S'only once in a lifetime.

CYRENNE. All gone. You've had it! There's fifty-five gone for a
burton.

PERCY. I shall put it all down to experience. Shove it in the out-
tray.

CYRENNE. Oh, you're not in the out-tray yet. In fact, you may
yet still be *outré*. (*She hiccoughs and giggles*) Pardon! I'm squiffy. (*She
moves to him and slaps his chest*)

(PERCY *falls backwards on to the bed; as he does so, his feet come up.*
CYRENNE *catches them, and we see two large holes in his shoes*)

Doesn't mummy have your shoes mended?

PERCY (*rising*) I've another pair at the digs, but brown didn't
match my suit.

CYRENNE. Darling Percival, I shall dance at your wedding. From
now on I'll sh—subscribe to the Scunthorpe *Bugle* or whatever's your
local rag.

PERCY. Scunthorpe's not in Manchester.

CYRENNE. All right, the Manchester *Bugle*. And as soon as your
wedding is announced, I'll catch the first train down—up. I'll find
your church, and when they're throwing confetti, with you on the
porch all flushed and tumbled, I'll shout "Oy!" (*She whistles*) "Remember me?" (*She opens her diary and writes*) "Percy came back!"
Exclamation mark!

(PERCY *takes the tray of dishes into the kitchen*)

PERCY. Bill Hedgers at the mill has a daughter sixteen and he's
only thirty-six. Must be wonderful to own someone like her while

you're still young: high heels, fluffy; someone you've made yourself. I envy him. Must be marvellous! Having her calling you "Dad"—asking your advice—must be marvellous! (*He picks up the pan and brush from under the sink*)

CYRENNE (*writing*) "Am going to tuck him up and take him on holiday."

(PERCY *has brought the pan and brush from the kitchen. Now he sweeps crumbs off the carpet*)

PERCY. I often imagine myself with a daughter, but never a wife. S'funny! I see myself as a widower; my wife has died young. I never bother how; she's just dead. This is on me long walks round town. I see myself with this baby: bathing it, and feeding it, and tickling it, and changing its nappies—I've never told anyone else this. Next she's off to school. I've got on by this time. I'm successful, important, grey round the temples—and I collect her in the car. One of those whoppers, you know, all wheels and straps round the bonnet. (*He takes the pan and brush back into the kitchen*) Then she comes home with her first boy-friend—and I start worrying! I have to shake my head and think of something else.

CYRENNE. Have you a dog at home, or a cat?

PERCY. No, why?

CYRENNE. It's something to love. (*She writes*) "Good old Ginger!!" Double exclamation mark. (*She snaps the diary shut*)

PERCY. What're you writing in there?

CYRENNE. The opening chapter of *Percy*, my latest book.

PERCY. I think you're marvellous. Phew! Poems and painting . . . !

(CYRENNE *picks up his jacket and helps him into it*)

What about the washing up?

CYRENNE. It's Sunday. 'Gainst the law to wash up on a Sunday. I heard of one man who did it and some of his dirty-minded friends never spoke to him again. (*She leads him* L)

PERCY. Where're we going?

CYRENNE. You must learn to ignore the tea-leaves till you need the pot again. (*She pushes him into the chair* L) You may've died by the next meal and you'd've wasted minutes of life round the dustbin. (*Kneeling* R *of him, she pulls off one of his shoes*)

PERCY. What're you doing?

(CYRENNE *takes off his other one, then rises and shows him the holes. She drops the shoes into his lap*)

CYRENNE. Once more around the block, dear friend, and you'd've been down to stocking feet. Now for slippers! I should have some.

(CYRENNE *exits down* L)

PERCY. Where've you gone?

CYRENNE (*off*) Rummaging for slippers.

PERCY (*suspiciously*) Men's slippers?

CYRENNE (*off*) What else?
PERCY (*darkly*) Whose are they?

(CYRENNE *enters down* L *with a newspaper, a pair of scissors, and
two paper bags*)

CYRENNE. Mr Green the Fruiterer's. (*She puts a bag on each of
Percy's feet and stands back to survey the result*) Mm. Very sexy! (*She takes
a cushion from the chair behind him, places it on the floor* R *of his chair and sits.
During the ensuing dialogue she cuts the paper and fits it into his shoes.
Casually*) Been on holiday this year?
PERCY. Yes. I went to Morecambe. Went with Ginger and his
wife'n kids. They have friends over there, you know. But I stayed
in digs.
CYRENNE. Otherwise all right?
PERCY. Yes, I had a marvellous time. Saw all the shows; did a
bit of swimming; and I went horse-riding one day; first time I've
done it. And there's some beautiful walks round there. One day I
went. . . .
CYRENNE. By yourself?
PERCY. Pardon?
CYRENNE. By yourself?
PERCY. No, I went with people from the digs. There were a lot
of married couples there. They took a fancy to me. I was always
making them laugh. No, it was marvellous! I think I'll go some-
where else next year, though.
CYRENNE. Good.
PERCY. What about you? Did you—I mean, do you. . . . (*He stops*)
CYRENNE. Yes, we're allowed holidays.
PERCY (*sorry*) Oh heck.
CYRENNE. 'S all right! Have you any more weeks coming?
PERCY. No, I've had my whack. Hey! Fancy you sitting there
doing that.
CYRENNE. Just fancy!
PERCY. Being domesticated. *You!*
CYRENNE. God help us, here we go again! Will you please stop
treating me like some sort of freak.
PERCY (*piqued*) Well, I'm sorry; but it's not one-sided you know!
If you stopped treating me like a yokel with straw hair and a patch
on me bottom . . . ! I shouldn't have said that. I'm sorry.
CYRENNE. Damn it, love, that's what I mean! If you feel like
saying "bottom", say it! We've all got one.
PERCY (*pompously*) The fact remains I do not consider it necessary
for a gentleman to be vulgar in the presence of a lady.

(CYRENNE *laughs helplessly, but* PERCY *remains on his dignity*)

If I accidentally make a blunt remark with a lady present, I apolo-
gize; I'll say no more.
CYRENNE. Next Sunday the Epistle of St Percy!

(*There is a silence, broken only by the snip-snip of* Cyrenne's *scissors.* Percy, *face set dogmatically, thinks over the past few sentences. Five seconds later a tiny smile twitches his lips. He kills it and has a quick look at Cyrenne. He thinks for another five seconds and the smile returns; he frowns hard in an effort to remain serious. This becomes impossible. He chokes back a chuckle; then another; and another.* Cyrenne *looks up, and he loses the battle*)

Percy (*between chuckles*) You aren't half rude! "We've all got one!" (*He roars with laughter*)
Cyrenne (*calmly*) Oh, I slay 'em.
Percy (*wiping his eyes*) Oh dear, oh dear, oh dear! (*He blows his nose*) I've had some real good fun tonight. I have!
Cyrenne. There you are, Killer! (*She gives him his shoes*)
Percy. Ta. Thanks very much. (*He puts on his shoes*)

(Cyrenne *rises and crosses to* R *to put the scissors on the dressing-table, and the paper in the waste-paper basket*)

Cyrenne. You know, love, you remind me of a paper bag.
Percy. S'funny thing to say.
Cyrenne. But you do. You remind me of a carrier bag; one of those old-fashioned ones with thick string-and-wood handles. Winthram's Drapery Store: brown and solid, until one day it carries a liberty bodice, and it crackles and giggles. Would you like to come on holiday.
Percy. Oh, aye! When do we go? Today?
Cyrenne. Yes, or tomorrow. (*She returns to sit on the cushion* R *of him*)

(Percy *laughs*)

Would you?
Percy. With you?
Cyrenne. Mm.
Percy. Nothing I'd like better.
Cyrenne. Will you come then?
Percy. Seriously?
Cyrenne. Very seriously.
Percy. I couldn't.
Cyrenne. The mill won't close without you.
Percy. No, but. . . .
Cyrenne. Afraid?
Percy. Me? Why should I be?
Cyrenne. Because of what mummy would say; and the boss; and the lady next door.
Percy. Did you mean for us—to go together, sort of—together?
Cyrenne. You'd be my Sunday boy, Percy. You'd have everything I've saved from the rest of the world. Just a week; no strings on my side. Then I'd wave you off at the coach station, and we'd both have something—well, something nice for. . . .

Percy. For when the eight o'clock buzzer goes!
Cyrenne. Will you come?
Percy. What about money? I'm not rich.
Cyrenne. Ginger's paying.
Percy. Eh? Oh, yes! (*He savours the idea*) Oogh, what I wouldn't give! See that plum in Ginger's mouth: it'd shrivel to a currant! (*He rises and moves* c, *shaking his head*) It's a cheeky idea. It is truly; but I couldn't possibly. I mean, it's winter. I've had my two weeks this year.
Cyrenne (*rising*) They weren't exactly a success though, were they? (*She moves to replace the cushion on the chair*)
Percy. Who said so?
Cyrenne. You did, between the lines.

(Percy *begins to bluster, then gives in and nods*)

Percy. I must be pretty obvious. It wasn't too good. Never is. I don't enjoy Christmas much, either.
Cyrenne (*moving to stand by him*) Well?
Percy. I'm trembling inside. 'Fact is, I don't have much confidence in myself, d'you follow? I've left it a bit late. I'm not thirty-five. I'm—I'm forty-two. Another six months I'll be forty-three. I don't think I could come up to your expectations. I know I *can't*. I'm not going on holiday to be ridiculed the first time we—if you'll excuse me—go into the bedroom. I'm being blunt, but there it is. (*He crosses her to up* L) You've arrived too late. You know how youngsters when they're growing up have pimples? Well, I had pimples—my face was covered in them. They lasted until I was twenty-six, and unfortunately I didn't have the right personality to rise above them. Then they suddenly cleared away—almost overnight. An Army doctor gave me a course of dieting. Very good man. So! I thought I'd be O.K. with girls at last. (*He shakes his head*) Believe me, I might just as well've kept the pimples. At least I'd've had an excuse.
Cyrenne. Supposing I told you—some of the things I say. . . . (*She bites her lip and stops*) Oh, take a chance, Percy! Why not? . . . Percy?

(Percy *swings to face her and the words tumble out*)

Percy. Because I'm afraid I'm not a man; I'm afraid I'm effeminate or something. Everyone I know's been married, and had children, and—I'm scared of finding there's something different about me. Oh, I know I should grab a chance to prove myself but —I'm afraid to. I'm afraid.
Cyrenne. There's nothing different about you, love. I'm the expert.
Percy. Oh, well, there's still the mill on Monday.

(Cyrenne *sits on the end of the bed, speaking more to herself than to him*)

CYRENNE. I wanted to go on holiday. I'd have liked to go to Switzerland; but anywhere would've done: Morcambe, Blackpool—Potter's Bar.

(*There is a pause.* PERCY *moves to her*)

PERCY. Have you a railway guide?
CYRENNE. Yes. Somewhere.
PERCY. Go and fetch it. We'll try Blackpool. (*He sits* L *of her on the bed*) I'll spend tonight at the hotel and bring my bag round first thing tomorrow. I've enough clothes for a week, if you don't mind rubbing through a couple of shirts for me.

(CYRENNE *nods*)

And would you not starch the collars, please? It cuts my neck.
CYRENNE. No starch.
PERCY. Oh, and a pair of socks, if you'd kindly rub through those, an' all.
CYRENNE. No starch!

(PERCY *laughs. Then summoning all his courage, he leans forward and pecks her cheek.* CYRENNE *responds by drawing his face close to hers; she kisses him purposefully and very professionally*)

(*Rising and crossing down* L) We'll buy some shirts. *I* need one or two things in any case. Now! Where is that timetable?

(CYRENNE *exits down* L.
    PERCY *sits for a long time thinking, and relishing her kiss. Slowly he relaxes. His optimism grows, then blooms into exuberance. He jumps up, slaps his fists, rubs his hands, laughs, cries, and at one point does a happy little shuffling dance, ending by swinging round in a circle. This movement brings him face to face with the bed. His confidence evaporates and he turns slowly away, frowning and biting the edge of his thumb. He walks to the dressing-table mirror and gazes at himself*)

PERCY. Oh, it'll be all right, lad. Don't worry. Just take it easy! I'll do it. I must. I will.

(*The telephone rings.* PERCY *answers it*)

Hello? (*He consults the number on the dial*) Yes? . . . Um, I beg pardon, sir? . . . Father? . . . *Whose* father? . . . Yes, righto. (*He hangs up and slumps on to the bed. He seems lost—dumbfounded*)

(CYRENNE *enters down* L, *an open railway guide in her hands. She crosses to* RC)

CYRENNE. This is printed in Latin, it's so old. Who was it?

(PERCY *does not reply*)

Darling, the phone! Who was it?
PERCY. It was your father, back from the dead.

(CYRENNE *stops in her tracks*)

CYRENNE. You mean my stepfather.

(PERCY *remains on the bed, his back to her*)

PERCY. When did your real father die?
CYRENNE. Long time ago. . . .
PERCY. And your mother married again!
CYRENNE. Yes.

(PERCY *rises and swings to face her. He is puzzled and angry because of it*)

PERCY. You said your mother died when you were twelve. (*He strides into the kitchen, switches on the light, finds her rent book over the cooker, and reads out the name from the cover*) "Miss C. Duponitrades."

(CYRENNE *moves* L)

Now it's making sense. (*He throws the book down, turns out the light, and returns to the bedroom*) Since when has there been a Greek brigadier in the British Army?
CYRENNE (*sitting down* L) Who said he was in the British Army?
PERCY. That man said he was your father—he talked with a foreign accent—said he was ringing from the café. Yes! Your father runs a café with your brother. Right!
CYRENNE (*defiantly*) Well done! Full marks.
PERCY (*pacing to* R *and* C; *angrily*) A rent book for a house you own; nannies and French marchionesses; an M.A. your father bought! Did you ever gᴏ to Oxford? Come on, the truth! Did you?
CYRENNE. I slopped in a dismal little kitchen from leaving school till I was twenty.
PERCY. And I swallowed it wholesale! Phew! Intricate details of parties on the river, and—and a brother-in-law who's a surgeon! And what about your mother? Is she alive, too?
CYRENNE. Yes, yes, yes, she's alive! Satisfied?
PERCY. That's something I'll never forgive. Your own flesh and blood—to say they were *dead!* That's awful. Aren't they good enough? Is that it? Just a little Italian couple, or Greek or whatever it is?
CYRENNE. I tried to explain once. Oh, it doesn't matter.
PERCY. Oh, no, it doesn't matter! It proves what a yob I am. Real gormless, that's me! You poked fun at everything I did. I couldn't even visit the bathroom without getting a belly laugh! But you were so clever, that's what gets me. I shed tears over you and your poor old brigadier—gave you five pounds to laugh at me!
CYRENNE. It was your own idea.
PERCY. I know; and I'll tell you another. You'll curl up at this. If the holiday had gone well I was thinking of marriage. You and me! Isn't that funny! (*He moves up* R)
CYRENNE. Oh, do me a favour, love! I know better; the first morning you'd have crawled off with your tail between your legs.

D

PERCY. Would I really?

CYRENNE. Yes, Percy.

PERCY. Would I! Would I! We'll see! (*He flings the cover off the bed*) I'm as good as you any time. I'm better!

(CYRENNE *makes no reply*)

What're you waiting for? More money? Get undressed!

(CYRENNE *turns to look at him, then slowly rises and crosses to the dressing-table*)

CYRENNE (*quietly*) All right. (*Deliberately she takes off her necklace and then her ear-rings*)

(PERCY *lowers his eyes and swings away, there are tears in his voice*)

PERCY. Oh, shut up and leave me alone!

(CYRENNE *moves up and leans on the tallboy up* R. PERCY *sits again, hunched on the* L *side of the bed*)

CYRENNE. You can't shame me—unfortunately.

PERCY. Everything's crumpled—just gone and crumpled. I had this feeling—wonderful—I thought you were so exciting—because I'm lonely. So damned lonely! Oh, what's the use! (*Rising, he takes his coat and scarf from the hooks and walks to the door up* L) I'd best be going. But I can't tell you how I wish I'd never answered that telephone.

CYRENNE. Would you like a heavenly chorus?

PERCY. Pardon?

CYRENNE. You could do a Charlie Chaplin down the middle of Euston Road: shuffling over the brow, the traffic lights blinking mistily. What a bloody fuss! (*Moving* RC, *she kicks off her shoes and shuffles into her slippers*)

PERCY. There's no call for swearing. It's not clever.

(*But the fish wife comes out in* CYRENNE)

CYRENNE. You come here in a stupor, find you've no guts, and you're ashamed—until I mention an M.A., a butler, and the fact I was sired by a brigadier.

PERCY. Yes, all lies.

CYRENNE. Listen, love, if I've told you the moon's green or God's a woman, I'm still the same person you appreciated ten minutes ago. So stuff that up your mill chimney! (*She takes off her stockings, resting each foot in turn on the dressing-table stool*)

PERCY. Oh, no! I'll not have that! You're not the same to me.

CYRENNE. Because you're a snob, a one hundred per cent, cast-iron, elastic-belted snob!

PERCY (*moving down* L) Not at all!

CYRENNE. Yes, you are, with your "Er by gums" and your "Up for the Cups!"

PERCY. Oh, sticks and stones!

CYRENNE. Your little British belly pumped with excitement at the thought of mixing with gentility, even to the extent of a gentle whore like me. (*She crosses* L *trying to unzip her dress*)

PERCY. Just—just watch your language!

CYRENNE. As soon as I establish a true-blue background you're thrilled and oh-so-terribly impressed.

(CYRENNE *exits down* L, *but returns immediately, moving up to him*)

You kiss my feet, cook my supper, and set up some kind of mission tent in my parlour. Unzip the back!

PERCY. What're you doing?

CYRENNE. Going to bed. What else? You use my flat and my time to bolster what's left of a tatty week-end; even go off and come back for more! (*She moves to the door down* L) Seven times round the block planning my redemption! But not once asking yourself if I care a pig's bottom what you plan.

(CYRENNE *exits down* L, *taking off her frock*)

PERCY. Oh, lovely! Lovely! Lovely words for a young lady! (*He moves up* R *and yells back across the bed*) Any planning that was done, you did! You planned me out of five quid *and* a holiday—at the end of which, no doubt, you'd have planned me out of everything else—premium bonds, the lot! (*He moves to the doorway down* L) I count myself very lucky—very lucky indeed! Are you listening?

(CYRENNE *enters down* L, *buttoning her pyjamas jacket. They are men's pyjamas of bright orange. She crosses to the dressing-table*)

CYRENNE. I don't give a galloping damn if you disappear in circles or hang yourself in your Lancashire cotton drawers. My life is my own! (*Deliberately she pulls off her right eyelashes*) And I live as I please. (*She removes her left eyelashes*) Every two-bit hero thinks he has a right to reorganize me. Bloody marvellous! (*She thickly covers her face in cleansing cream, then removes her make-up with tissues*)

PERCY. I've asked you to watch your lang——

CYRENNE. There's the door! Nobody's keeping you. Go on! Slam it and shout, "Bum" through the keyhole!

PERCY. By heck! (*He leans against the door up* L)

CYRENNE. There's one comes round here. I'll tell you! Once a week I hear him creeping down the steps; I hear him breathing while he's prising up the letter-box flap—to shout through it—to scream and slobber filthy words at me.

PERCY. Well, he's to be pitied.

(*The slanging match is over. They are both calm now*)

CYRENNE. The lies I tell are useful to me. They're old friends, the people I invent. I laugh with them and cry with them. You think you are lonely? You've a mummy back home waiting to pack your rattle and fold your scarf all ready for next year. I bet she's baking a cake this very minute. And what about *your* father?

PERCY. He works at the mill.

CYRENNE. Old pals together! On one of my birthdays I was admiring myself in the mirror; wasn't wearing much. My stepfather came in without knocking. After an unpatriotic incident I won't bother to shock you with, I left home. (*She rises*) Are you with me so far, Padre?

PERCY. Yes.

(CYRENNE *sits on the* R *side of the bed and kicks off her slippers*)

CYRENNE. You see, my stepfather, well, he wasn't a good step-daddy—(*She clambers into bed*) so, I started pretending I was someone else's daughter—usually a character in the book I was reading. I was always reading. I read *What Katy Did* and what she did next. Oh, I swallowed the lot, from Dickens to *Lady Chatterley*—at which point, Padre, I gave up reading. I examined my assets from the front, back, to the side, and I said, "Cyrenne! You've struck oil!" (*She plumps her pillow*) Next comes a dismal romance lasting one year and two days, and ending with my fiancé in jail for slashing his wife—the wife he hadn't mentioned. He still writes to me, complaining about the food. Then I was a nurse, then a typist, shop assistant, hostess, and finally—well, as for the rest of my saga—I deserve a bloody M.A.! (*She hurls a spare pillow at him*) So!—now and then I lunch with Lady This or That, spend twenty pounds an ounce on Woolworth's fragrant scent, or race down Oxford lanes with my dashing virgin boy. And when the going's rough, the brigadier is there with lovely tales of Samarkand or Rumblejumble-pore. No, I don't give a toot what anyone thinks. I have a goddam wonderful life. So Good night, Children, Everywhere! (*She flops back and draws the sheets over her head*)

PERCY. Phew! You don't half cuss! Bet you could beat Ginger if you really tried.

(CYRENNE *rises and, without looking at him, goes into the kitchen.* PERCY *follows to* RC. CYRENNE *gets a glass of water and returns. She passes Percy with a sniff, demurely holding the collar of her pyjama jacket, and makes a wide circle around him, getting into bed at the* L *side*)

CYRENNE. I thought you'd gone back to Scunthorpe.

PERCY. It's Manchester; you know perfectly well.

CYRENNE. Oh. (*Placing the glass on the bedside table, she snuggles under the sheets*)

PERCY. They suit you, those pyjamas. You look quite nice. (*He clears his throat*) As I said before. . . .

CYRENNE (*muffled*) And you'll say again!

PERCY. I beg your pardon?

(CYRENNE *sits bolt upright and looks at him with a heavy sigh*)

CYRENNE. Are you coming to bed or aren't you?

PERCY. Eh?

CYRENNE. You heard.

(PERCY *opens his mouth several times, then changes his mind. Finally he turns and looks at her. She smiles slowly—a friendly, kindly smile. He grins sheepishly in return. Everything looks very promising—then suddenly he loses the mood and sits hopelessly on the* R *edge of the bed*)

PERCY. Oh, I don't know. I'll have to think about it.

CURTAIN

BREAKDOWN OF THE TELEPHONE CONVERSATIONS

ACT I

CYRENNE (page 17)

CYRENNE. Yes?
BILL. Hello, Cyrenne-sweetheart!
CYRENNE. Hello, Willie-darling!
BILL. Darling yourself. How's tricks?
CYRENNE. All right; and you?
BILL. Got a cold.
CYRENNE (*laughing intimately*) Well, you shouldn't run about with nothing on.
BILL. You suggested it.
CYRENNE. I did no such thing.
BILL. Strip poker was your idea.
CYRENNE. Oh, no! It was your idea. (*To Percy*) Don't break anything, will you, love.
BILL. Say that again?
CYRENNE. I wasn't talking to you, Willie.
BILL. Is someone there?
CYRENNE. Yes. Jealous?
BILL. Madly. Who is it?
CYRENNE. Mind your own business!
BILL. Feel like a party tonight?
CYRENNE. Go to a party *tonight?*
BILL. Yes. Now. Pronto!
CYRENNE. What sort of party?
BILL. You'd turn up a trip on a yacht?
CYRENNE. Yacht? What kind of yacht?
BILL. A real yacht. Lap lap.
CYRENNE. I've never been to a party on a yacht.
BILL. Weakening, Sweetie?
CYRENNE. Hang on! (*To Percy*) Do you really want to stay?
PERCY. I don't want to stop you having . . .
CYRENNE. I asked you if you wanted to stay.
PERCY. Yes. But I mean . . .
CYRENNE. Whatever happens?
PERCY. How d'you mean?
CYRENNE (*smiling, then speaks into receiver*) No go, Willie! My boy friend won't let me.
BILL. Which boy friend?

PERCY. No, wait a minute!
CYRENNE. Ssssh! (*Into phone*) What did you say?
BILL. Which boy friend?
CYRENNE. Oh, he's just a fellow who does the washing-up. G'bye.
(*She replaces the receiver*)

ACT II

PERCY (page 26)

PERCY. Hello? Is that the Pablo Private Hotel, please?
VOICE. It's the Pablo. Yes, that's right.
PERCY. Oh. This is Mr Winthram. Has Mr Grappley returned yet, please?
VOICE. Grappley? Dunno. I'll find out.
PERCY. Thank you. (*To himself*) Fighting time now; and I'm too damn scared to wind the clock . . . Oh, what if he's not back? What if he's plastered down some alley?
GINGER. Hello?
PERCY. Hello, Ginge! It's Perce.
GINGER. Speak up!
PERCY. *Perce.*
GINGER. Hello, love! How'd you make out?
PERCY. Fine. I got on fine.
GINGER. Did you do it?
PERCY. I er, came *home* with her, yes.
GINGER. I know; but you're not still there?
PERCY. Yes.
GINGER. Bluddy-'ell! What've you been doing?
PERCY. Talking.
GINGER. *Talking!* Is that all?
PERCY. It's all so far, yes.
GINGER. Ha ha! Get your wallet!
PERCY. Ginge, listen! Don't you think it's a bit stupid, all this?
GINGER. Ha, I've won! No backing out!
PERCY. I'm not backing out at all. Frankly I'm giving you a chance. I mean, I'm here. I'm *here*, Ginge! Just a matter of time, that's all . . . Hello?
GINGER. I'm here.
PERCY. D'you still want to go through with it, then?
GINGER. You've lost! You're done! You're dead scared! (*He hangs up*)
PERCY. Who's dead scared. Ha! . . . Hello? . . . Hello? . . . Ginger? . . . (*He hangs up*)

CYRENNE (page 34)

CYRENNE. Yes?
BILL. Cyrenna-mia?
CYRENNE. Yes.
BILL. It's Romeo, sweetheart!
CYRENNE. Willie-darling, hello!
BILL. We're just starting out.
CYRENNE. Starting out for where?
BILL. For the yacht, sugar. Change your mind and come.
CYRENNE. No thanks, love. I've been on the *Queen Mary*. (*Urgently*)
Come round here instead.
BILL. And miss free champagne?
CYRENNE. *Please*, Willie. *Please*. Come and see me, Willie. *Please*
come over.
BILL. Sorry. It's me for the *Skylark*.
CYRENNE. You'll be seasick.
BILL. Come with me, and we'll bring up the past together.
CYRENNE. Yes. (*Dully*) Some other time. (*She hangs up*)

ACT III

PERCY (page 44)

PERCY. Hello?
PAPA. Bays-a-water seven-seven-nothings-seven?
PERCY (*checking number*) Yes?
PAPA. I am wishing-a speak-a to Ricky. Yes? No, no? Tell-a
Ricky, pliss. Papa is-a waiting.
PERCY. Um . . . I beg pardon, sir?
PAPA. Ah! Is-a not Ricky. Ohkay! Pliss to ring later. Yes?
Am-a the old father. Papa Duponitrades.
PERCY. Father?
PAPA. Si-si.
PERCY. *Whose* father?
PAPA. Cyrenna is-a my daughter. She's the good girl. Am speak
from the café. Yes? Ohkay? Will ringa later. Bye-bye. Ohkay? (*He
rings off*)
PERCY. Yes, righto. (*He hangs up*)

FURNITURE AND PROPERTY PLOT

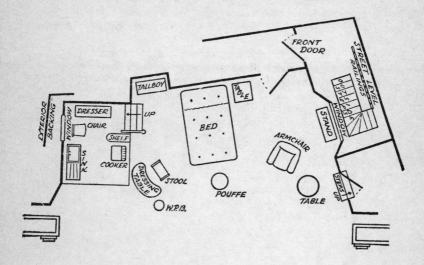

ACT I

On stage : In the kitchen:

Window with lace curtains

Gas cooker (with electric element fitted, to boil kettle)

Shelves above cooker, with tea-caddy, etc., and gas meter on
   the top shelf

Vegetable rack, plate-drying rack

Sink and draining-board with shelf beneath

Cluttered dishes, pots, pans, etc.

Cutlery box with knives, forks, spoons

Shelf above sink (with cup-hooks) and tinned foods, bread,
   butter, cheese, sugar; transparent biscuit box, etc.

Ascot water-heater

Practical taps (with rubber piping to tank behind)

Kitchen dresser

Chair

Pedal garbage pail

Bottles, etc., on the floor

Linoleum

Three steps with a miniature banister rail lead down to the
   bedroom level

In the bedroom:

    Carpet and rugs
    Dressing-table and stool (down R)
    Record-player on the floor (down R) and records
    Electric fire on the floor (RC)
    Waste-paper basket (down R)
    Tallboy (up R) with books, etc.; whisky bottle
    Three-quarter divan bed (C) with dressing
    Pouffe on floor below bed
    Bedside table with lamp, radio, ashtray, telephone and
       directories
    Door (up L) with mortice-lock and clothes-pegs
    Light switch R of door (with card pinned above it)
    Window (L) with bars on it; and curtains
    Ornamental stand for plants in window alcove
    Armchair LC with cushions
    Coffee-table beside armchair, with ashtray and magazine
    Door (down L) with clothes-pegs (two steps lead up to it)

Set: *In the kitchen:*

    Kettle and teapot on cooker
    Tea-caddy on shelf above cooker
    Box of matches on cooker
    Towel on draining-board
    Squeeze-in soap on draining-board
    Pan and brush under the sink
    Rent book on hook above sink
    Cheese, butter, sugar on shelf
    2 biscuits in tin
    Tray (with 2 cups, knives and plates, near to hand)
    2 tumblers on dresser
    Apron on dresser
    Milk bottle on floor near dresser (empty)
    Milk bottle on draining-board (half full)

On dressing-table:

    Brush and comb, hand mirror, etc.
    Cleansing cream
    Diary and pen
    Razor
    Foreign stamps in bowl
    Perfume, powder bowls, etc.
    Cigarettes and matches

On tallboy:

    Whisky bottle on top
    Newspaper on top
    CYRENNE's (brightly coloured) blouse in top drawer
    Tissues in top drawer

Bottle of aspirins in second drawer
White jewellery box in second drawer (with chain medallion and
    bracelet)

On the bed:

Toy dog (or nightdress case similarly shaped)
2 pillows, sheets, blankets, etc.
CYRENNE's slippers beneath downstage end
Transistor radio on bedside table
Cigarettes on bedside table
CYRENNE's black négligé hanging on door (up L)
Key in lock of door (up L)
Spare key planted on floor RC (in case original is lost)
Window curtains open
Lights and switches off

Off stage down L: CYRENNE's black trousers

Personal: *For* CYRENNE:

Handbag and key
White raincoat, low-cut satin cocktail dress, black bra and
    waist slip, shoes, ear-rings, stockings, etc.

For PERCY:

4 pennies
Wallet with £5 note
Wrist watch
Handkerchief
Card with telephone number
Squashed cigarette packet (and bent cigarette)
Rattle
Scarf and rosette
Raincoat, blue suit, cardigan, collar-attached shirt with tie,
    socks, and shoes with holes

ACT II

Check: Radio on bedside table
       Diary on bed
       Jewellery box on tallboy
       Newspaper on tallboy

Off stage: CYRENNE's blue dress and gold necklace

Personal: *For Ricard:*

Cigarette case
Lighter

Signet ring
Bow tie, raincoat (over shoulder), dark flashy suit, striped
shirt, socks, shoes, etc.

ACT III

Set: *On floor below bed:*
       Tray of used dishes, cutlery, etc.
       2 glasses
       An orange
       Whisky bottle (from dressing-table)
       Cushions
    Tidy kitchen
    Hang PERCY's raincoat behind door up L

Check: Tissues on dressing-table
       Diary on bed

Off stage (*down* L):   2 paper bags, newspaper, and scissors
                 Railway timetable
                 CYRENNE's orange pyjamas

LIGHTING PLOT

Property fittings required: 2 pendant lamps, 1 bedside table lamp, 1 electric element on top of gas cooker to boil kettle

Interior. A bedroom and kitchen. The same scene throughout

THE APPARENT SOURCES OF LIGHT are pendants up C and in the kitchen up R, a table-lamp up LC, a street-lamp outside the window L, and moonlight outside the kitchen window R

THE MAIN ACTING AREAS are C, RC, LC and down L

ACT I.   Night

To open: Room in darkness
Moonlight coming through kitchen window
Street light through bedroom window
Fire off

Cue 1   CYRENNE switches on bedroom light   (Page 1)
Snap in bedroom pendant
Snap in covering lights

Cue 2   CYRENNE switches on table-lamp   (Page 2)
Snap in table-lamp
Snap in covering lights

Cue 3   CYRENNE turns on electric fire   (Page 2)
Bring up fire

Cue 4   CYRENNE switches on kitchen light   (Page 2)
Snap in kitchen pendant
Snap in covering lights

Cue 5   CYRENNE switches off kitchen light   (Page 2)
Snap off kitchen pendant
Snap off covering lights

Cue 6   PERCY switches on kitchen light   (Page 10)
Snap in kitchen pendant
Snap in covering lights

Cue 7   PERCY switches off kitchen light   (Page 12)
Snap off kitchen pendant
Snap off covering lights

Cue 8	CYRENNE switches on kitchen light *Snap in kitchen pendant* *Snap in covering lights*	(Page 16)

ACT II.   Night

To open: Lights as at close of previous Act

Cue 9	CYRENNE switches off kitchen light *Snap off kitchen pendant* *Snap off covering lights*	(Page 23)
Cue 10	CYRENNE switches on kitchen light *Snap in kitchen pendant* *Snap in covering lights*	(Page 32)
Cue 11	CYRENNE switches off kitchen light *Snap off kitchen pendant* *Snap off covering lights*	(Page 32)
Cue 12	PERCY switches on kitchen light *Snap in kitchen pendant* *Snap in covering lights*	(Page 36)

ACT III.   Night

To open: Lights as at close of previous Act
             Kitchen off

Cue 13	PERCY switches on kitchen light *Snap in kitchen pendant* *Snap in covering lights*	(Page 45)
Cue 14	PERCY switches off kitchen light *Snap off kitchen pendant* *Snap off covering lights*	(Page 45)

EFFECTS PLOT

ACT I

Cue 1   At rise of CURTAIN   (Page 1)
          Car door slams and taxi drives away

Cue 2   CYRENNE turns on record-player   (Page 2)
          Quiet music

Cue 3   CYRENNE turns off record-player   (Page 2)
          Music off

Cue 4   PERCY: ". . . I see."   (Page 11)
          Kettle whistles

Cue 5   CYRENNE turns off gas   (Page 11)
          Whistle off

Cue 6   CYRENNE: "Use the towel you had before"   (Page 17)
          Telephone rings

Cue 7   CYRENNE: "Come on, Man! I'm waiting."   (Page 18)
          Loud dance music on radio

Cue 8   CYRENNE clicks radio off   (Page 18)
          Music off

Cue 9   CYRENNE turns radio on   (Page 18)
          Dance music

Cue 10 CYRENNE turns radio up to full   (Page 18)
          Increase volume

ACT II

Cue 11 At rise of CURTAIN   (Page 19)
          Dance music on radio

Cue 12 PERCY: "Sorry."   (Page 19)
          Music ends and foreign announcer heard

Cue 13 PERCY switches off radio   (Page 19)
          Announcer off

Cue 14 PERCY: ". . . this time I could."   (Page 27)
          Doorbell rings

Cue 15   PERCY: ". . . be friendly again."   (Page 27)
             Doorbell rings

Cue 16   CYRENNE: "I don't need anyone."   (Page 34)
             Telephone rings

Cue 17   CYRENNE sits on stool   (Page 34)
             Doorbell rings

ACT III

Cue 18   PERCY: "I must. I will."   (Page 44)
             Telephone rings

Character costumes and wigs used in the performance of plays contained in
French's Acting Editions may be obtained from Charles H Fox Ltd, 25
Shelton Street, London WC2H 9HX